PORSCHE 356
Guide to Do-it-Yourself Restoration

Jim Kellogg

ISBN 0-929758-23-4

Published by Beeman Jorgensen, Inc.
7510 Allisonville Road, Suite 123, Indianapolis, IN 46250 U.S.A.

Printed and bound in the United States of America
Cover design by Llew Kinst, Cupertino, California

Porsche, the Porsche Crest, Carrera, Targa and the distinctive shapes of the Porsche
models are trademarks and trade dress of Dr. Ing. h.c.F. Porsche AG.

First Printing, March 2004

Contents

This book is dedicated to Barb, my wife of thirty years. Who else would allow me to make significant noise and great smells in the basement below her kitchen? JBILYVM

And in memory of Dave Lindeman — Back when I was writing restoration articles for the Rocky Mountain 356 Porsche Club newsletter, I thought about creating an award to recognize an individual who undertook and completed a 356 restoration. The first award would have gone to Dave Lindeman. Dave rope towed his 356 find home from a car lot in Denver. He did the entire restoration, including the engine rebuild and paint. When finished he drove his 356 the way it was meant to be driven — fast. I never got around to the award and Dave went to wait for Ferry Porsche in March 2000. Dave, you did a great 356 restoration!

Introduction

This book is about restoring a 356 Porsche to driver level condition. The focus will not be to spend time or money creating the perfect 356. For example, it is often not necessary to search for NOS (new old stock) replacement panels, if a reproduction panel or patch is appropriate. A concours winning restoration is not the goal, but rather a restoration that will be correct, admired and driven.

The information in the *356 Porsche Technical and Restoration Guide* will not be repeated in this book, but some of its contents will be recommended for reference. The *Guide* is a compilation of technical articles originally published in 356 Registry magazine and is available from this publisher and most 356 Porsche parts suppliers. When this book is referred to, it will be called the *Restoration Guide*.

This book does not contain details on engine or transmission rebuilding. This information is available in a variety of excellent publications that you also can find via the vendors link at www.356registry.org.

This book will provide a detailed step-by-step approach to restoring a 356 Porsche. The reader should have some mechanical skills, but need not have previously attempted a restoration. There will be some cost alternatives offered and a few stories mixed in. Most of the procedures described here will be for a coupe. Differences for other models are described in *The 356 Porsche, A Restorer's Guide to Authenticity* by Dr. Brett Johnson. You must have this book. It will be referred to as *Authenticity*. *Authenticity* can be continually referenced to determine your specific 356's characteristics. It also is available from this publisher and most 356 Porsche parts suppliers.

In addition to the *Restoration Guide* and *Authenticity*, you should also obtain the following:

- Owners Manual
- Workshop Manual
- Parts Manual

These books are available from various 356 vendors. Reproductions are available at lower cost than the original publications.

There also is a video called *Made by Hand* which was filmed at the factory in 1961 and is only available from the 356 Registry Goodie Store. This is very informative and should be viewed. Everyone laughs when they show the undercoating technique.

Also, if you do not yet own and are considering purchasing a 356, you must read Jim Schrager's *Buying, Driving and Enjoying the Porsche 356.*

Chapter 1

Preliminary Steps

Congratulations! You have decided to restore a 356 Porsche. You will find this to be a very enjoyable learning experience. Prior to disassembly, determine the scope of your project. If the car is in boxes because a previous owner started disassembly, at least the previous owner saved you some work; however, you may have difficulty assembling your project, since you did not remove the parts. If someone else disassembled the car, some parts may be missing and some of these may be hard to replace.

We purchased a really nice disassembled 1961 Roadster with no collision damage and minimal rust. This would be a shop car, one we would restore and sell. We did a complete inventory and all the parts were there. Later we discovered the very good seats were from a later model and would not work since the seat rails are different.

If your 356 project is in one piece whether running or not running for years (typical), the first thing to do is take a lot of pictures of the outside of the car. Months later when it is time to ask, "Where is the rear script for the car?", it will be easy to see if it was there in the first place. Pictures of how the windshield rubber seals and trim fit on a 356 are also important. Start a project notebook for notes and drawings in addition to pictures you will take throughout the disassembly process.

Removing Gasoline

Before putting the 356 into the shop or garage, check the fuel tank. There are two types of gas tanks: early (1950-61) and later (1962-65). On both types, remove the gas cap and smell. If there is a strong varnish smell, it is old gas or old gas residue. The tank will have to be cleaned. On the early tank, use a flashlight to determine if there is gas in the tank. On the later 356, put your ear to the filler and jiggle the car. For safety, it is necessary to remove the gas. Before doing so, contact your local fire department for guidelines on disposal of gasoline.

Turn the gas lever under the dash to *ZU*, which is closed/

off (*AUF* is open/on). The petcock lever on early 356s points down in the *AUF* position (up on later 356s). In both cases, turn counterclockwise to close the petcock.

Early tank procedure: Turn the petcock off (*ZU*). Remove the rubber fuel line from the fuel petcock inside the car that goes to the steel line in the tunnel. It may be very tight and it may have to be cut. Don't worry, all fuel lines will be replaced during restoration. Buy a 6-foot length of 5/16 inch fuel line and a hose clamp at an auto parts store. This line will reach from the petcock to outside the car. Attach the hose to the petcock, secure with the clamp, use an appropriate catch can and turn the petcock to *RES* for reserve.

Appropriate catch can for removing gas from early tank

Late tank procedure: Buy a 4-foot length of 5/16 inch fuel line at an auto parts store. Turn the petcock off (*ZU*). Go to the engine compartment and remove the fuel line to the fuel pump. Insert the 5/16 fuel line between the rear engine tin and chassis by pushing the rubber seal back. Attach the fuel line to the metal fuel line from the gas tank. Place the other end in a suitable container on the ground.

Removing gas from later 356

What a 6-volt Optima battery looks like; the 12-volt has six cylinders and is twice as big and heavy.

Chock the rear wheels. Jack up the front of the car using a thick piece of wood, i.e. 2 x 10 two feet long under the battery box. Turn the petcock to *RES* (reserve). A small amount of gasoline will remain in the tank, so turn the petcock to *ZU*. There are other methods of removing gasoline from the tank, but this approach will work. We once quickly stopped someone who was using a wet/dry vacuum-really!

Checking Electrics

Next it is good to check the conditions of the electrics. This can be a difficult area if previous owners have made modification. A new battery is recommended. It will probably be six volts but you may have a later 356 or one that has been converted to 12 volts. Check this by inspecting codes on the generator. A code of 160/6 or 200/6 included in the generator part number indicates 6 volts (and 160 or 200 watts). Twelve volt generators have 14v in the part number.

Early 90 watt, 6 volt generator.. Note this number is located at the end next to the fan shroud.

The Optima battery is preferred by owners of later 356s as it is sealed and does not leak acid in the front battery compartment. It is offered in six and 12 volt configurations and is widely available. The Optima battery has excellent starting amperage and a long shelf life; however, it requires different mounting provisions for various 356 models. These are described on the 356 Registry web site.

After this first electrical check, the battery will be good to use during the reassembly phase. Don't worry about storing the battery on the floor; that rule applies only to the early tar covered batteries.

A ground strap should be found in the front compartment. It may not be in the proper position, but don't worry about that now. If not present, buy one that is 12-18 inches long from any auto parts supplier. The ground strap should be grounded to the body of the car with a bolt and washer. Sandpaper can be used to find the clean, shiny metal necessary for the connection. You also may have to use a piece of plywood to keep your battery in the compartment, if the car has substantial rust damage.

The wires that attach to the positive pole of the battery are the heavy black wire which goes to the starter and the smaller black or red wire that goes to the ignition switch. These will be in the center or left side of the compartment. There should be a terminal clamp on these wires to attach the battery. If missing, it is available at auto parts suppliers.

Connect these wires to the positive pole of the battery first. Then touch your ground strap to the negative pole. There should not be a spark. If there is, something is turned on like a light switch. Check all the switches on the dash; they should be pushed in and the ignition switch off and the doors closed. If all appear off and you still get a spark, you will have to abort the test until later in the restoration process as you have a short and it will be easier to find as electrical parts are evaluated later. If no spark, connect the ground strap to the battery but leave it so you can hand twist it off. Look for any smoke. If everything is okay you can start testing the electrics.

We have always recommended that the battery ground strap be secured to the battery just tight enough so that it can be rotated and pulled off by hand. An alternative is a battery disconnect. One of our neighbors drove his 1964 electric sunroof coupe to the shop to visit. It started to drizzle so he closed the sunroof and came inside. After about five minutes, we returned to his 356 and it was full of smoke! "Quick!" I yelled, "Pop the hood!" He did and I twisted off the ground strap. Checking on the problem, the headliner was hot. We found the problem! The sunroof switch for the electric sunroof is an open rocker switch under the dash. A small pebble was lodged in there and held the switch open. His 356 did not have an original sunroof; it had been "clipped" (i.e. cut) from another 356. When this was done, a fuse for the sunroof was not installed. I told my neighbor he had a problem since his sunroof motor was probably burned up and they are very hard to find. I also told him how and where to install the special sunroof fuse. He called the next day and said his sunroof motor was okay and everything still worked. We call this "keeping the 356 faith."

Testing the electrics is straightforward and all that needs to be done is to check functionality and collect notes on what works and doesn't. If you are not familiar with the electrical switches on a 356, refer to the owner's manual. The headlights, horn, cigarette lighter, dome light and clock will work with the ignition off. Take notes on what works and what doesn't. Try the horn, windshield wipers and headlights. Check the license light. Try the dimmer switch and headlight flasher. To flash the headlights, pull back turn signal stalk (1960 - 1965) or push the horn button if you have a horn ring which honks the horn (1956 - 1959).

With the ignition switch on, there should be a red and green light on the left most gauge (combination gauge), if the 356 is 1958 or later and the engine is installed. The oil temp needle should move from its rest position to the bottom of the green area. Don't worry about the fuel gauge now. Try the turn signals. With a broomstick or a friend try the brakes. Put the car in reverse and check the back up light. If there is oil in the engine, see if it will turn over. Do not try to start it. That's it. You now have good notes on what worked before the restoration was started.

General Conditions

With the doors, hood and rear lid shut, check to see if they fit flush. Check with a straight edge. Are the gaps uniform? Probably not, but don't worry; remember this is just getting a feel for the scope of the project. Check the door latch function. This will be used a lot later when using the door as a jig. If the latch seems to hang up, it will need to be cleaned and operation checked after removal. Try the window operation.

Checking door fit with a straight edge.

This front door gap is uneven.

While this rear gap is fairly even, it is not flush to the rear fender. This might be adjusted by moving the striker plate inward.

Try the keys in the different locks, which vary by model, i.e. ignition, door, glove box, hood latch and shift lock. Mark each key for its function. If keys are missing, they can be obtained from a special vendor mentioned later. You can lock the door with the key or by pushing up the

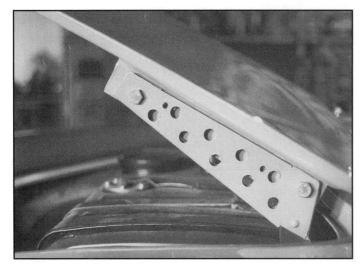

The two small holes are the index holes for the front hood hinge.

Chassis serial number location in the luggage compartment.

interior door handle. If you leave the key in the car, push up the door handle and shut the door; you are locked out unless you have a spare key. There may be keys for the shift lock (if present) and hood release on open 356s. Make a note of which keys you have and which you need.

Open the hood and rear lid; there should be index holes drilled through the hinge and the hood/lid. If the hole is straight through (seldom happens) and the hood/lid fit well you are very lucky. If not, it will be fixed later. Check

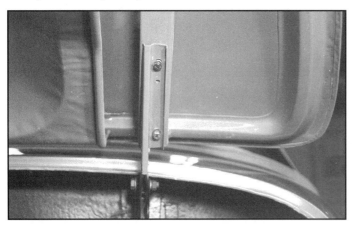

An index hole for rear lid. There may be none, one or two.

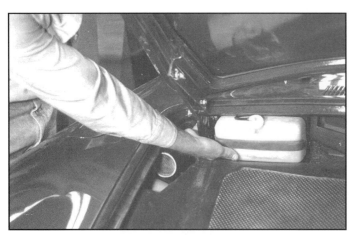

Tripping the hood hinge star wheel by hand.

the hood hinge operation. It is necessary to lift the hood to close. Does it go up and down easily or do you have to trip the star wheel on the hinge with your finger? After 40-50 years, this hinge may need rebuilding. This will be done later. The hood may also be *kinked*. This is damage at the hinge area due to forcing the hood to close rather than lifting it first. Some interesting and perhaps ugly repairs may have been done in this area.

Chassis Number Check

The chassis (VIN) number is stamped into the center section of the chassis below the gas tank and above the battery box area. It will be under a rubber mat or a plastic cover above the spare tire strap fastener. It will be four to six numbers about an inch high. On early 356s there is also an aluminum tag about 1 1/2 inches by 5 3/4 inches riveted to the chassis below the side of the gas tank on the right (passenger) side. It should have the serial number stamped on it along with other data, including the date of manufacture. On later 356s an aluminum tag with the same information is riveted to the left of the chassis serial number in the center section. There also are one or two ID tags on the left door hinge cover. It will have the chassis number and

Aluminum identification tag in the luggage compartment.

4

Close-up photo of the ID plate

Last two digits of chassis serial number on left hinge blade. We have seen a few on the right hinge blade.

Coachbuilder ID tag with chassis number in the left side door hinge cover plate

maybe the paint code, stamped on small aluminum tags riveted to the hinge cover.

The doors, hood and deck lid were originally fit to each individual car using lead to create uniform gaps. These parts were stamped with the last two or three digits of the chassis serial number and then removed from the body and placed on a separate dolly while the car was painted. After paint, the numbered parts were reinstalled on the correct car. This can be seen in the movie *Made by Hand*.

On the inside of the hood on the left hinge blade, there should be two or three numbers stamped in corresponding to the last two or three numbers of the chassis serial number. If not there, don't worry, many 356s encountered front-end damage and the hood may have been replaced. While the hood is up, look for dates on the early gas tank. This is the black rectangular tank; the later flat tank may have a date code, but it can only be seen when the tank is removed. There should be a month and two-digit year date on the lower right ledge of the early tank. Also, on top of the tank, except for cars built prior to 1954 (Speedsters prior to 1956), is the silver colored sending unit. It has two wires connected to it. There should be a

month and year stamped on it. Early 356s used a stick to measure the gas level rather than the sending unit and fuel gauge.

There should be two or three numbers stamped in the upper right corner under the rear grille, or on the male part of the rear lid latch. These are the most common areas. The number may be on the lower back of the lid on occasion. There are also on a few lids various two character codes like G3 stamped in the upper left area of the lid opposite the serial number. To date, research has not yielded the purpose of this code. If you can't see the numbers on the rear lid they may be painted over and they will be visible after the lid has been stripped. Rear lids are seldom replaced as they pop up in rear collision.

With the rear lid up, check the engine serial number. It will be different than the chassis number. You will probably need a strong flashlight and a rag. The number is stamped on the vertical piece of the case above the lower pulley and below the generator stand (1955-65). It should start

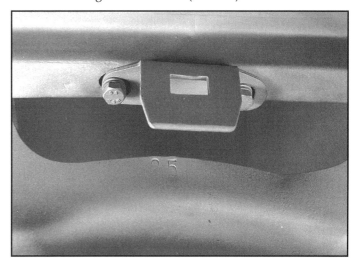

This rear deck serial number is in an unusual location.

out P (star) and then six numbers. If you see KDP before the number, it is a factory rebuilt engine. If the number is not present, the engine case could have been replaced. If the number appears to have been ground off, you could have a problem proving originality of the engine. If the number is there, write it down, along with the chassis number. To verify if the engine was original to the 356, you'll need to get a *Certificate of Authenticity* from Porsche Cars North America (PCNA). The current procedure to obtain the Certificate of Authenticity can be found at the 356 Registry web site. It may take weeks, even months, to receive the certificate, but it will tell, if the engine number is original to the car and it also may contain a transmission number, interior/exterior color and options fitted. This is also referred to as *Kardex* information.

We were evaluating a 1963 B Coupe but something was strange. It had disc brakes and a C dash. The chassis number and ID plate were for a 1963 B, the chassis number on the hinge cover matched. The registration was for a 1963. So we decided to check the hidden chassis number. On some of the later 356s, this was stamped on the chassis behind the right door hinge cover. We removed the three small screws and the number there was for a 1964! We surmised the 356 could have been stolen and the thieves had pieces and paper from a wrecked 1963 or perhaps a previous owner with a parts car just found it easier to replace the number rather than jump through hoops at the DMV. They did a real nice job of welding in the chassis number, but they didn't know about the hidden number. The owner was disappointed, but his plan was to make it a race car and he promised to divulge the problem if he sold the 356.

Chapter 2

Disassembly

Required Tools

Tools used in this chapter are basic shop tools: metric wrenches, metric socket set, screw drivers (Phillips and flat), utility or X-acto knife with extra blades, locking pliers, hammer, drift, awl, metric tap and die set, floor jack, jack stands and flashlight. You also need to get some penetrating oil. If the car was built prior to mid-1955, the Phillips screwdriver won't be necessary.

When we surveyed those we had coached on 356 restoration with the question, "What is the best advice we gave you?"

They replied, "Your recommendation to get a metric tap and die set." The tap and die set is a collection of tools that allow you to clean the threads on male and female fasteners. If you don't want to get a complete metric tap and die set, you will find an 8 x 1.25 and 6 x 1.00 tap/die will chase most of the hardware threads on a 356. This is a job that can be done while watching TV and will speed up reassembly.

More Preliminaries

Disassembly of a 356 can take between forty and eighty hours. The key words in disassembly are *never throw anything away*. Parts that are in poor shape can still be used as patterns.

The first step in disassembly is to disconnect the battery. Next remove the seats and take pictures of the interior. To remove the seats, there is an adjustment lever on the lower outside of the seat. Pull it up or outward, depending on the model, and push the seat forward. It should come off the rails. Remove the passenger seat first; it is easier. If it doesn't come off the rails, it could be hanging up on the rubber and aluminum tunnel cover. Hold this down while holding up the lever and pushing the seats. Three hands are needed for this, so find a friend or remove the tunnel cover.

To remove the tunnel cover, first remove the front floor mat. A 10 mm open-end wrench can be used to pop the control rod off the accelerator pedal. When removing the mat, be careful not to damage the fuel petcock on early 356s. If the mat is in good shape, be careful around the pedals not to tear it. Unscrew the shifter knob. Loosen and pull off the shifter boot. Pull up and remove the tunnel cover; it should clear the heater knob/lever. Now the seat should slide forward and off the rails. If the driver seat hits the steering wheel, you may be able to recline the back of the seat by pulling on the lever at the seat hinge if it is present.

Popping off ball socket on gas pedal.

With the seats out, replace the shifter boot and knob. Store the tunnel cover if it was removed. Now, take pictures of the interior. Include how the (hopefully) original carpet is installed and how the dash is laid out. Shoot as much detail as you think you will need.

We had disassembled numerous 356 coupes and got out of the habit of taking pictures. This bit us when we were reassembling

Kroil penetrating solvent, Extend and Anti-Seize

a Karmann Hardtop we had restored. The way the carpet and interior trim were assembled was completely different than a regular coupe. The quarter window trim was also different. So the advice for any first time (and probably second, third, . . . time) restorer is to take plenty of pictures throughout the process.

Here are a few more valuable disassembly tips. Some parts were marked right (R) and left (L) at the factory and some are interchangeable (like front hood hinges) and are unmarked. Other things, like door window regulators, are unmarked, but must be marked as they are interchangeable, but only work on the correct side. The tip is to mark everything right or left as it is removed. You can use a scratch awl on metal parts that will be blasted or dipped, and tape and indelible ink on others.

The next tip is to keep the hardware with the part. If you remove a hood or lid hinge, mark it right or left and then put the bolts, nuts and washers back on the part.
To remove parts you should use a penetrating oil. WD-40 is not a penetrating oil; it is a water displacement (WD) lubricant. There are many penetration oils and each has its proponents. We use Aerokroil, manufactured by Kano Laboratories (www.kanolabs.com). We first used it on a 1957 Speedster stored outside in Denver weather for over 20 years. We were able to remove every nut, bolt and screw without damage. Another product often used is Liquid Wrench.

Before using penetrating oil, clean the area with a small wire brush. Let the penetrating oil do its thing; a few hours or overnight is best. When removing the fastener with socket, wrench or screwdriver, an old mechanics trick is to tighten a little bit first then remove. If the fastener starts to squeal, stop; it is getting ready to break. Apply more penetrating oil, loosen and try later. Sometimes it will be necessary to use heat to remove a fastener. A propane torch should be sufficient.

When removing parts, bag them and then box them by area. Zip lock bags in various sizes work well. Use a permanent marking pen to label each bag as right door parts,

front compartment parts, dash parts, etc. You can sort parts for repair or replacement later as you sit in front of the TV and use your metric tap and die set on the hardware. You should box all chrome plated parts separately as you will have to decide to clean, buff, replace or re-chrome them.

Jacking Up the 356

While it is not necessary to jack up the 356 yet for disassembly; you may need to for other reasons. Never use the original jack points below the doors!

To remove the wheels, loosen the lug nuts with a 19 mm or three-quarter inch socket with extension before using the jack. To jack up a 356, a floor jack should be used to do it safely. Jack up the rear first. Before jacking up, chock the front wheels so the car doesn't roll forward. Slide the floor jack under the engine and place the cup of the jack under the transmission hoop. This is a curved hoop that secures the transmission to the chassis. You will be able to see the bottom of it. With the rear of the 356 jacked up, place jack stands under the torsion tube. This is the large tube in the front of the transmission directly behind the rear seat area. Use jack stands rated for the weight of the 356, at least 2,000 pounds.

To jack up the front of the 356, place a two-foot long piece of 2 x 10 lumber on the jack and place under the battery

Floor jack positioned under transmission hoop. Note orientation of bolts/nuts.

Jack stand under torsion tube.

8

Jack stands with notched tops will secure the front of a 356 at the sway bar mount without damage. Flat top, not recommended.

Floor jack with 2 x 10 wood under rear of battery box and jack stand under sway bar mounting bracket.

box to lift. Place your jack stands where the sway bar has mounting points. The sway bar is the long rod behind the battery box that connects the lower control arms. All 1954 and earlier 356s do not have a sway bar. Jack stand placement is in the same area, directly under where the lower control arm enters the chassis.

Door Disassembly

Now start taking the 356 apart. So far the seats are out and maybe the tunnel cover. Start with a door. Now is the time

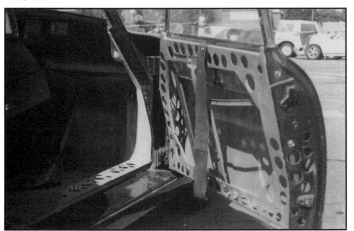

This door has few parts. It is on a 1951 steel bodied factory race car that has never been street driven. In 1982, at Monterey, the owner met the Porsche technician who drilled and champhered these holes and many others. He asked him how did he know how many holes to drill. The technician said, "We keep drilling until we beat the Ferrari."

to refer to your Workshop Manual. A door has a lot of parts; you will need to take good notes and photos! It is easier to disassemble the door while it is on the car. You should have already checked and noted door and window operation during the check on general conditions.

The first items to remove are the interior door handles and window cranks. First push back the plastic escutheon and you'll see a pin securing the handle to the regulator. If you look closely you will see the pin doesn't go through the middle but is off to the side. Use an awl, small punch, ice pick or nail to drive out the pin. Make sure you are clear of the escutheon so you won't damage it. With the pins removed, the handles can be removed by pulling toward the center of the car. Both handles come off the same way.

Next, remove the door panel. Two screws and finishing washers hold the top piece, called a garnish rail or door cap, then multiple screws and finishing washers around the periphery. The door panel should come off. If the panel has an armrest, lift up and off on later cars. Behind the panel should be a piece of plastic to keep moisture from the upholstery. There might also be a piece of carpet that acts as a sound deadener for the door.

Now check the number on the door. It should be in the middle somewhere and two to three digits matching the

Removing the interior door handle pin.

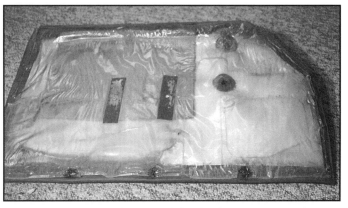

An original door panel removed for the first time. Note the plastic protection and the large piece of carpet. Two metal brackets secure the early style arm rest. Three drops of tar were used in the bottom holes for the screws and finish washers.

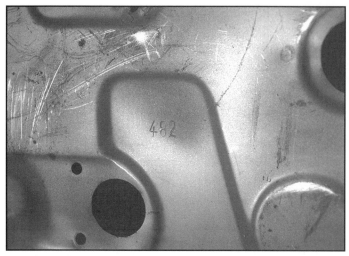

Serial number on the inside of a door. Usually found in the center, they have been observed in other locations.

last few numbers of the chassis number. Only on Roadsters, built by the Belgium coachbuilder D'Ieteren, will you find the door number on the bottom of the door. You don't have to take off the door panel to check!

You will find two rubber seals on the front and rear edges of the door. Note how they are oriented and glued on. It will not be obvious when you install replacement seals, so take more pictures. Take off the seals using a putty knife;

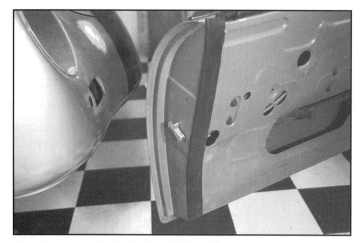

Rear door seal. Note that it is high at the top.

Front door seal. Often there is a screw and finish washer at the outside of the V. Note also that the hinge pins have not yet been seated on this 356. Protect the painted area with tape when doing this.

Bottom door seal. Note how the drain notches in the rubber seal go to the inside

save them for a future pattern. In fact, save all rubber seals for patterns. On later 356s, there may also be a seal on the door bottom, although this is often missing. It has notches that are open to the drain holes in the door bottom.

Now is the time to make a diagram of the door and all the bolt locations. Some bolts will have thin heads so they won't mar the panel. As these bolts are removed, note their length and location on the diagram.

The first big piece to remove is the chrome window frame. This may or may not include a vent window for the coupes. Cabriolets later than 1958 will just have the vent window. Early cabriolets, Roadsters and Convertible Ds have just inner window channels and Speedsters nothing. The coupe window frame is secured by two bolts behind the holes in the front of the door that is covered by the rubber seal. A deep socket is needed to remove them. On coupes there will be one or two special bolts securing the frame at the back of the door.

Now the bottom and brackets. Leave the brackets inside the door secured to the door bottom if it is not rusted. They provide alignment for the window frame and will provide a starting point during reassembly. The bolts securing the brackets to the window frame will probably be rusty and are in a difficult location to reach. Penetrating oil, a flashlight in the door and perseverance will do the

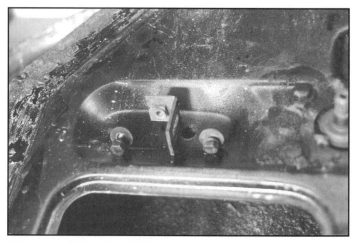

The vent window bracket is secured inside the door.

10

The wheels on the regulator have springs to hold them tight to the window frame

trick. There is also a bolt and bracket below the vent window, if present. The window frame will pull out but you have to clear some welded reinforcing tabs on the sides.

Next remove the glass. The glass is bonded to a grooved frame at the bottom. The frame rides on the wheel(s) of the regulator. Use your window crank to check the operation, but be careful as you don't have the frame to guide the glass. The regulator on Convertible Ds, Roadsters and cabriolets differs from coupes in that it is secured to the glass frame in front by a circlip, bolt, spacer and nut. The nut is behind the frame, not visible but must be removed. You will have to loosen the regulator and let it drop to the bottom of the door, in order to slide the glass off the regulator. Protect the glass for storage with newspaper/cardboard and tape.

Remove the regulator. Attach the bolts/washers after removal so they don't get lost. Mark the regulator right and left as they will go in either side but only go up halfway if on the wrong side. Oops! Lying on the floor could be a plastic profile about four inches long. This is a seal between the bottom of the vent window and the door. Bag it; it is needed for reassembly.

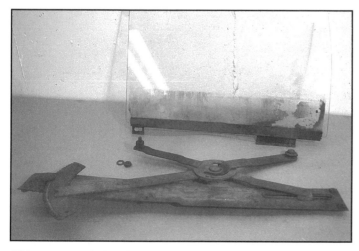

This 356 was obviously painted with the window in the door.

Now remove the top chrome piece and profile. The screw heads are buried in that black fuzzy strip. There may be rust in this area and you want to remove the screws without enlarging the screw holes. You can get to the screw end inside the door with a small channel lock plier if needed. Next you can remove the door latch. On early 356s, this is attached to the interior door handle operator by a long flat bar and is removed as one unit. The screws for the latch and bolts for the operator are easy to find. On later 356s, the latch is secured to the operator by a pull wire secured in the operator by an allen screw and on the latch by a cotter pin and very thin washers. Remove the latch and operator and all that is left is the exterior door handle. It is secured by a screw and washer(s) at the front and slides forward for removal. There is a rubber buffer at the bottom front of the door. It is difficult to remove due to rust. If it looks OK, leave it in place and cover with tape.

The door is now disassembled and ready for stripping. Take a minute and inspect the area that was behind the panel. You may find interesting marks made at the factory. In fact inspect all the parts as you remove them for interesting marks. Some you can puzzle over like the R and L marks on the aluminum hinge covers. It is obvious which is right and left. Why were they marked?

Next remove the door at the hinges. The first parts off are the aluminum hinge covers. They are secured by three screws, two of which may be hiding behind the rubber door seal. On the back of the hinge cover at the bottom will be the serial number and perhaps right or left markings. The door should be removed at the hinge pin rather than removing the four bolts on each hinge. Clean the pin area and use penetrating oil. If the hinge has a zerk (grease fitting) for lubrication, remove it. The top pin is the hardest. Remove the cotter pin and washer if present. With the door all the way open, use a long drift (tapered rod) and strike the end of the pin. Use a good size hammer. Be careful not to flare out or mushroom the end of the pin. Hopefully, the pin will move, get it flush with the top of

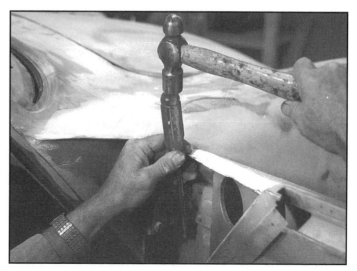

Using a hammer and screwdriver to drive out the upper hinge pin. There is a notch cut in the blade for this application.

the hinge. Now move to the bottom pin. Under the pin should be a small round rubber plug. Remove it. You can now insert your drift straight up from underneath and drive up the pin. Go about halfway and return to the upper pin. Use your drift or long screwdriver on the head of the pin and drive it almost out. Return to the bottom pin and drive it out leaving the drift in the hinge. Next, support the door with a friend or milk crate and drive out the top pin with a long screwdriver. Jiggle the door and remove the drift from the bottom door. Remove the door.

Door disassembly sounds simple, but it's not. We are talking about 40- to 50-year-old parts that may never have been disassembled. On the later 356s, the factory changed the hinge pin design which made it harder to remove. Early hinge pins had a spiral grove that matched up to a zerk that could be greased. Later 356s had no zerk, just an oil hole and the pin was straight with notches at the pinhead to really hold to the hinge.

On later 356s, we got into the habit of removing the doors at the hinge and then driving out the pin with the door off the 356. Sometimes we would have to drill out the pin when big hammers and heat wouldn't work. On B.J.'s '64 coupe we removed the door and got the drifts, big hammers, propane torch and bandages handy. B.J. hit the top pin with a drift and it came out on the first blow. So did the bottom. B.J. said, "Dad, this 356 is talking to us. It wants to be restored." And so they will. All throughout the disassembly process the 356 will talk to you. Some nicely, some not so nice.

The story brings up a point; when things aren't going well or as expected, it's time to walk away and take a break. There is no reason to get frustrated; remember this is supposed to be an enjoyable learning experience. While you are taking a break, a new solution to the problem will probably occur to you.

If you have to remove a door via the bolts and it fit well, be sure to count and record the number of shims behind each hinge. Scribe around the hinge as much as possible

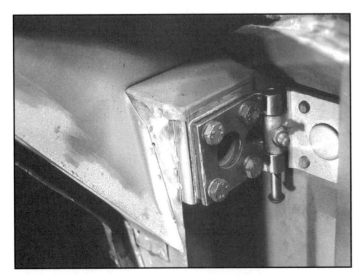

Here there are three shims behind the hinge. One appears to be home-made as it is too big. Shims are 1 or 2 mm.

before removing the bolts. If you remove the door via the bolts, you will have to spend a lot of time later repositioning the hinges and door before metal repair. The door is going to be used as a jig and it will come off and go on many times using the pins. If you had to remove the door via the bolts, clean your removed pins, ensure they go into the hinge easily and reinstall the door. With the door disassembled, use a curved carpet knife or similar tool to clean out any caulk or debris at the inside bottom seam (assuming it hasn't rusted away).

Hood Removal

Moving on to the hood. It is removed by the two bolts at each hinge. These should be 14 mm across the flats (ATF). Often these are a mix of 14, 13, 12 mm ATF indicating the original bolts were lost during previous hood removals. Since 14 mm ATF bolts are no longer available, the 356 is talking nice to you if it has a lot of 14 ATF bolts. If the index holes lined up during your pre-disassembly inspection, the hood is not kinked and the numbers match, feel very lucky. You have a virgin hood, which is very rare! More than likely you will have to repair the hood. With the hood off, scribe with an awl around the male latch and remove it. Now you can remove the hood handle. Note the washers on the studs. There should be a rubber/plastic gasket(s) between the hood handle and paint. In fact, except on very early cars (1950-51), wherever an external part i.e. headlight, taillight, door handle was over the paint, the paint was protected by a rubber or plastic gasket.

When we are at a 356 event and participate in people's choice balloting, we have a trick to sort out the T6 B and C cars. We check where the hood handle is secured in front. There should be two rubber washers there. You can barely see them and they are usually missing on T6 cars that have been restored or had the hood handle replaced. This inspection can reduce the T6 voting pool to a reasonable number. Usually, the T6 car that wins people's choice does not have these rubber washers. Oh well!

Gas Tank Removal

While working in the front compartment, remove the empty gas tank. On early 356s it is secured by two straps in the front compartment and the lever and hose to the fuel petcock inside.

First, remove the two wires, if present, to the fuel sending unit. Push the wires back into the interior to get them out of the way. On the early tank, make sure the lever is turned to ZU and remove the fuel lever from the petcock by removing the cotter pin. Remove or cut the hose from the petcock to the tunnel tube, if not done previously during fuel removal. Remove the two 14 ATF bolts securing the straps. Push the straps down. Pull the gas tank up and out, being careful not to hang up the petcock.

For the later tank, removal is more complicated. Turn the

Later tank fuel petcock. The tie rod is hiding the fuel hose connection to the tunnel line. Part of the cotter pin can be seen.

At the top, the short hose from the tank that connects to the long L tube that goes through the gaskets and is held by chassis clips. To the left, the chassis gaskets. In the center, the rubber collar, clamp and drain channel. The curved rubber hose is the drain from the filler area. Four clamps and bolts that secure tank to chassis.

fuel lever to ZU. Remove the plastic gas tank cover if present. Loosen the lug nuts on right front wheel. Chock the rear wheels and jack up the front using thick wood under the battery box floor. Secure with jack stands under the front sway bar brackets. Get under the car and remove the cotter pin securing the fuel lever to the petcock. Take a flashlight with you and wear eye protection. Push the fuel lever back into the car. Remove the fuel line from the petcock; you may have to cut it.

Next remove the right wheel. Look up in the fender to locate a bracket that secures the neck of the gas tank to the chassis. Also note a metal tube that connects to the gas tank vent hose. There is also a rubber collar and drain channel going up into the filler area. Two screws secure the bracket through the chassis under the fender. Remove them. There should also be two screws inside the front compartment securing a similar bracket through the chassis. Remove them. Next remove the rubber vent hose that goes from the tank to the metal tube. It should pull off and be re-useable, but you may have to cut it. Also remove the wires to the sending unit. On early T6 cars, it may be a bottom sending unit. Now back under the fender, remove the metal vent tube. It is secured by four fold over tabs.

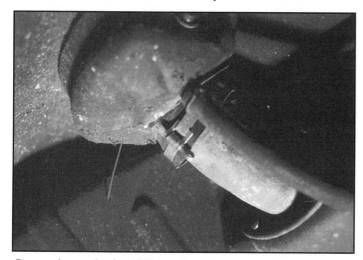

Connection at the fuel filler and gaskets to the chassis.

Use a screwdriver to remove the undercoat and pry them up. You should be able to pull the tube out. Now pry the bracket up onto the gas tank neck. You will see there is also a rubber gasket. Pry it back also. Now remove the clamp that holds that rubber collar. You may have to cut it to get it off. It is replaceable. Loosen the rubber collar by twisting on the bottom and pushing down with a blunt tool from the gas filler area. As it comes loose, a metal drain channel piece may fall out. With the bracket, gasket and rubber collar loose on the neck, remove the four 14 ATF bolts and clamps securing the tank to the chassis. Note or photograph the orientation of the clamps.

Remove the gas cap. You can now remove the tank. You may have to carefully pry up on the tank as it has a tendency to glue itself to the insulation material. Pull the tank up and toward the front and left side, clearing the petcock through the opening; stop when the neck is close to the chassis hole and remove the collar, bracket and gasket from the neck. Note the orientation of brackets and gasket for future installation. Pull the tank out, take outside to vent and you are done.

On both tanks remove the fuel petcock as it or the tank can get damaged as you move it around. Carefully remove the fuel bowl on the petcock. It still may be full of gas. There may also be crud in the fuel bowl. This will indicate the condition of the tank and whether the fuel petcock should be replaced or restored.

Front Compartment Parts

It is now possible to remove the rest of the parts in the front compartment. On the early 356s, all that is left is the hinges, washer bag and ID tag. The hinges will be removed later after taking off some parts from the dash. Removal of the washer bag is obvious. The ID tag, which is found along the side of the tank, is riveted in place. There may be a smaller tag that says *Modell 1959 or 1960*. Yes, that's the way it is spelled. Place tape over the heads of the rivets. Get inside the car and look for where the rivets were peened down. A little light sanding should reveal

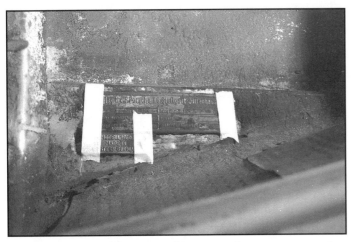

Protect the rivets with tape so they are not lost upon removal.

This later rear bumper has a *spinner* at the bracket and a missing captive nut at the end.

their location. Use a dremel or rotary tool to remove the peened end of the rivet. Then use an awl or ice pick to carefully tap the rivet up. Remove the ID tag(s) and replace the tape if the rivet damaged it. The ID tag(s) will be restored later and then attached with epoxy cement to the freshly restored interior compartment using the original rivets and rivet holes.

For the later 356s, remove the fuse cover and washer container. On the 356B cars (except Roadsters) there is a plastic drain box, drain tube and the fresh air cans. The box is secured by two L shaped brackets with bolts. Once the bolts are loosened, the brackets will pivot and the box can be pulled down and out. The drain tube attaches to a metal tube that goes down through the door hinge cavity. It can be pulled off. The ID plates up front are pop riveted and these can be drilled out for removal. The fresh air cans are bolted to the inner fender panel. Use a wire brush to thoroughly clean the nut. Soak with penetrating oil as this stud and nut have a tendency to break. With the nut off and the cable from the dashboard disconnected, the air can can be pulled to the side to clear the stud, then wiggled out of the two rubber tubes.

Rear Lid Removal

Next move to the back of the 356 and remove the rear lid and grille(s). The rear lid is secured to the hinges by four bolts. These are easily identified and removed. With the lid on the workbench, the grill is either attached by machine screws/nuts (early cars) or small bolts/nuts (later cars). You may have to use a small wrench (15/64) from an ignition wrench set to remove the nuts. The grille(s) are a tight fit but should pull out. There is a rubber/plastic gasket underneath on all but the very first 356s. The rear hinges can be removed by the bolts at the top of the hinge pocket. Note the orientation of the bolts. Also note there is a right and left hinge; mark them.

Bumper Disassembly

The bumpers will be removed as a unit and disassembled on the workbench. On the early cars, the bumper brackets slide into a channel along with a bar with threaded holes for the bolts. On the later cars (1960-65), the channel has welded nuts inside and the brackets are attached to the outside with bolts. The later rear bumpers are also secured to the fender brace with a bolt, large washer and two large round rubber gaskets with a metal sleeve. The bracket bolts can be difficult to remove as there is usually damage in this area, particularly the fronts; use your penetrating oil and try not to shear the bolt or break loose the weld nut. This is particularly true for the end bolts on the later bumpers. Take your time; the bumpers will come off.

With the bumpers on the workbench, it is easy to see how to remove the bumper guards. The rear bumper guards may or may not have the exhaust through the bumper guard with attached funnel. On the 1958 and 1959 cars, the aluminum exhaust funnel is pressed into the bumper guard and it is extremely hard to remove. Leave it. On the later bumper guards, the formed sheet metal funnel, if present, is secured by a nut and small bracket. All the nuts and bolts securing the bumper guards and brackets will be difficult to remove. Use your metal brush to clean threads and your penetrating oil. When you are removing the bumper brackets you may discover a *spinner*. This is a bolt that rotates but doesn't come out since the weld nut in the bumper has broken loose. You can try to jam tools in between the bracket and bumper but this seldom works. Just grind the bolt head off; you will need to replace the weld nut later. (Check the section on tools if you are not familiar with grinding tools.)

The deco strip is the last piece to come off the bumper. These nuts will also be rusted tight. If you are planning on replacing the deco strip, which is the usual case, just snap off or grind off the nuts with a dremel tool and carbide cutting wheel. If the decos are in good shape, they can be restored. The aluminum trim on early 356s is easier to restore as it is not anodized. You start with 120 grit sandpaper and work up to 360 grit and then buff on buffing wheel. OK, the bumpers are bare and ready for stripping. They are difficult to store as they are always falling over. You might consider a long shelf or brackets on the wall or maybe suspend them from the ceiling.

Interior Parts

First decide if you need to remove the instruments and dash parts. If the paint on the dash is in good shape and the car will be painted the same color, why disassemble the dash? Maybe just freshen it. Your call; just an option to consider. On the other hand, if the gauges need to be rebuilt and switch hardware needs to be chromed, you might as well take it apart.

Steering Wheel Removal

To remove the instruments, it is best to first remove the steering wheel. On all 356s, the horn button has to come off to access the steering shaft nut. On early 356s (1950-59), look behind the steering wheel, you will see two small holes; these allow you to push the horn button out. But first carefully clean around the chrome edge of the horn button with a thin knife blade. Then use penetrating oil around the chrome edge. Find a long nail or rod that will fit into the hole; make sure it has a blunt tip. Insert in the hole and gently tap, alternating holes. The horn button should come out. Secure it loosely with tape so it doesn't fall off and break. If this procedure doesn't work, you can remove the steering wheel and shaft and work on it on the

Using a blunt hex key to tap the back of the horn button secured with tape.

Above the round steering coupler is the bolt with keepers. Part of the notch is visible to insert screwdriver. Note the steering shaft is not centered in the tube and must be adjusted. Yes, this is a right-hand drive 356.

workbench. To do this, remove the inspection cover in the front compartment. You will see a U bracket and bolt/nut securing the steering shaft to the steering coupler (the rubber disk). Carefully inspect the steering coupler. It is a round rubber disc. If you see cracks of deterioration, make a note for replacement. Obviously, it is very critical for safe driving. There is also a metal keeper on the U bracket that folds over to secure the nut. Use an awl to scratch the position of the steering shaft on the coupler shaft. Bend back the keepers and remove the bolt/nut U bracket and keeper. You can use an old screwdriver and penetrating solvent to drive the steering shaft off the coupler shaft. The steering shaft and steering wheel can then be removed to the workbench. Once the horn button is off, a rubber cup is revealed. This will pull off. It provides the rebound to the horn button, and if hard and inflexible (usual case), it will have to be replaced. The steering shaft nut and washer can be accessed to remove the steering wheel.

Only once were we defeated in removing the horn button. This was on an early car that also had a horn ring. With the assembly on the bench, we just could not push off the horn button. We finally had to pry off the horn button damaging the chrome ring. The problem was there is a metal cup in the steering wheel that allows attachment of the horn ring. The cup has two holes that should line up with the access holes on the back of the steering wheel. It had been installed wrong in the past and the holes were blocked.

If you have a horn ring, note that the cup is attached with three electrically isolated machine screws. There also is a foam ring that will probably have to be replaced, which provides the rebound for the horn ring.

On the later 356s (1960-65), the horn button has three ears. You push down on the horn button and use the ears to turn counter clockwise. This is a metal to metal connection; you may have to use some penetrating oil. With the

Steering shaft and wheel on workbench. The small round object is the rubber cup that provides horn rebound and often needs replacement.

Instrument brackets and knurled nuts.

horn button off, you can remove the rubber cup and access the nut and washer and remove the steering wheel.

Dash Disassembly

Now you get to spend some time on your back under the dash. A thick blanket or cushion will help. Looking behind the instruments, you will see two knurled nuts securing a bracket. Remove the nuts and bracket and the instruments will push out. Now take careful notes and diagrams of which wire goes where. In the past all we had were these notes when we reassembled the instruments. The factory wiring diagrams were not very helpful. But today, thanks to Joe Leoni of 356 Electrics, detailed drawings exist of the instrument wiring of all 356s of all years. Not only the instruments, but all the wiring on the cars. Wires are attached to the instrument by bulb holders with screws or bullet connections. Both just pull out from the instruments. Be careful pulling bullet connectors. Pull them straight out, gently. Use penetrating oil if necessary.

Once an instrument is removed from the wires, it is fun to check the back of it for date stamps, stickers from a previous rebuild or even the name of someone who worked on the instrument. There is a wire with bulbs to illuminate all the instruments. It is connected to the light switch. It is best to remove this bulb string as the bulbs will get broken if left in the 356.

After the instruments are out, switches can be removed. Most knobs are turned counter clockwise for removal. The

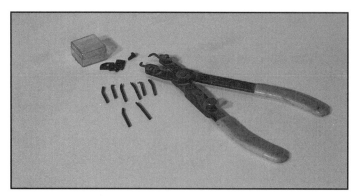

The special pliers with various tips for different applications. The right angle tips work well to remove the chrome switch bezels on the dash.

chrome bezels have holes on the side for a special tool. Sears sells snap ring pliers with removable tips, including some right angle tips, that work on unscrewing the bezel. If you are careful you could try a wooden skewer cut down to a few inches and lightly tap it. Ice picks and awls are not recommended. Wiggling the back of the switch as you turn the bezel often helps. Some switches have a nut behind the dash to position the bezel. We usually leave the switch attached to its wires, protecting it with aluminum foil and duct tape.

On early 356s (1951-55), there is an oil temperature gauge with a capillary tube; this must be removed at the engine and pulled through the tunnel and then the instrument and tube pull out of the dash. Some 1954 and earlier 356s may also have a pneumatic tube for the gas gauge that runs to the tank. It must be removed at the tank. Some 356s have a hand throttle, which is connected to a special pivot at the accelerator pedal. This must be removed at the pivot and the unit pulled out of the dash. This can be a real bear of a job as there is not much room down in the tunnel. You may want to wait until you remove the floor boards and pedal cluster discussed later. The knob on the unit may or may not be removable.

Removing the radio should be obvious. One or two small screws may hold the knobs on or they may pull off. There is usually a support bracket to the back of the radio. Wires usually pull out; there may be a fused connection that twists apart. With the radio out, you can get to the clock. Your 356 (1962-65) may have a fresh air/heater/blower control above the clock. You have to remove the nuts behind the dash to pull it forward to access the circlip and cable clamp. Be careful removing the nuts because the cable attached to the control is curved and puts tension on the unit. It is easy to break the stud on the unit. Leave the cables under the dash.

The fresh air/gas heater/blower control has two slots. There will be a lever in the top slot if the car was fitted with the optional blower and/or gas heater. The bottom lever controls the fresh air flow.

Leave the wiper motor in place if the wipers were working during the general conditions check. Remove the wiper arms and rubber grommet, and cover the wiper shafts with duct tape. If the wipers weren't working, remove the wiper motor noting rubber isolation washers and wiring connections.

If the car has a glove box, it is removed by two long screws with a strap connected at the top and bottom of the box. These long screws simplify installation. Early 356s have six perimeter screws securing the glove box.

Steering Column Removal

With the steering wheel off, the steering column can now be removed. On early 356s, there may be one or two elec-

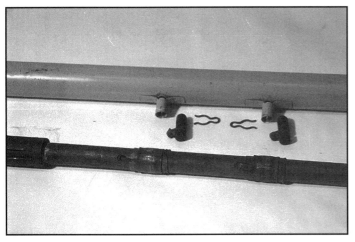

An early steering column and shaft showing the contacts and clips for the headlight flasher and horns. The contact area is on the shaft and the wires run through the shaft to connect to the horn ring and button. If there is no horn ring there would be only one contact and contact area.

trical contacts inserted into a holder on the steering column. These are for the horn and headlight flasher. Remove the clip and pull out.

The steering column is held to the dash by a removable clamp. The nut or nut plate is under the dash. Removing the clamp allows the steering column to drop down a bit. Now you need to remove the wires from the turn signal switch. You will see that there are many wires that go into rubber connectors with two female ends. Pull out the wires that come from the turn signal and leave the connector on the corresponding colored wire under the dash.

The steering column can now be pulled out. It is sealed by a rubber doughnut on the bulkhead. This may come out or remain in place when you pull out the column. If you previously removed the steering shaft, you should replace it and attach the steering wheel to move the 356 as needed. Just support the steering shaft with a wire loop where the clamp was.

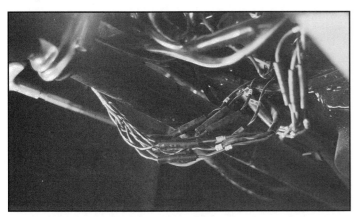

The wires from the 1960-65 turn signal switch go to the same color wires in the main wiring harness via a female/female connector. The tags on these wires indicate a replacement wiring harness. They are incorrectly installed; they should be over the top of the column, secured to the chassis by a fold-over clip

The emergency brake can be removed by disconnecting the cable from the pivot assembly in the front compartment via the inspection plate opening. It helps to pull the pivot assembly forward and place a small block of wood behind it to get some slack on the cable. Removal of the retaining pin is obvious. Once the cable is detached, the whole emergency brake unit can be removed after unfastening the two nuts on the front compartment floor by the hinge area. Removal of the emergency brake on early 356s is similar, but there is a bowden tube that holds the cable in a curve. Refer to your Workshop Manual for removal.

Windshield/Dash Removal

To remove the front and rear windshield, it is necessary to sacrifice the rubber seals. Start with the front windshield. Using a utility knife with a fresh blade, cut the seal inside about midway. You will see a slight groove in the rubber. Cut around the top and sides. With the dash still in, it is difficult to cut the bottom. With the rubber removed, press in the upper corners with the flat of your hand. The windshield should move and start to come out. If not, cut some more rubber. It's possible a previous owner had sealant put around the seal, so proceed slowly and carefully. If you can reuse the windshield, you are saving $400-$550.

The rear windshield is removed the same way, but use a new blade in the utility knife. Rubber quickly dulls a knife blade. The only injury we have had in 10 years was due to a dull blade. There is a technique that involves getting on your hands and knees inside the 356 and giving a mule kick to the rear glass. You have to have someone catch it as it flies out. While this technique is effective, it is not recommended for the first timers. The rear glass is tempered making it stronger than the front, which is laminated.

Leave aluminum trim and remaining rubber on the glass pieces for storage. Store them on edge, not flat. If the trim is good enough for reuse, don't remove it as it can easily get bent out of shape (1956-65 coupes and cabriolets).

With the windshield out, dash top removal is easier. If there is a light in the center of the dash top it will pull out and you can disconnect the wires. Screws under the dash top secure it to the dash. Remove them. You will have to remove the rubber seals around the door opening as the dash top upholstery material is folded and glued under them. The rubber seal should pull out as it is held by friction, small tabs and glue. Just pull from the rear and/or push from the front and the dash top will slide out. You will see how it is attached by angled tabs that fit into slots. The 1950 through 1955 coupes and cabriolets have a removable dashboard secured at the ends by two bolts and an aluminum spacer or wire filler strip.

Quarter Window Removal

The quarter windows are removed by the four small machine screws and special nuts that can been seen at the

The special hex nuts for the quarter window and the tricky cuts for the seal over the hinges.

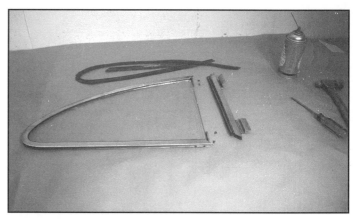

The small and often stubborn screws that secure the corner brackets to the frame.

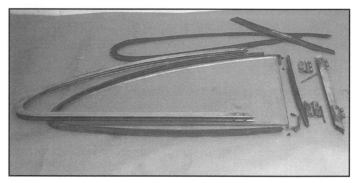

The hinge part on the vertical frame piece usually cannot be removed..

hinges. A 7 mm wrench will hold the special nut, and the screw head is visible with the door seal rubber removed. The three screws that hold the rear latch also have to be removed, but put them back in the holes as their location will be required, when the headliner is installed. The quarter window seal pulls out. Note that it is not glued. Note also right and left as they will be used as patterns to trim new rubber. If the quarter window just needs a new outer seal, it is easily replaced. However, if you need to replace the inner seal between the glass and chrome frame or you need to re-chrome the frame, disassembly can be difficult. The problem is the L shaped brackets and screws that hold the frame together. The screws may shear off requiring precise drilling and re-tapping. Thoroughly clean and use penetrating oil before attempting removal. If damaged, the brackets and screws are available. Note a slight difference in the angle between top and bottom brackets. Mark for correct reassembly.

The interior mirror is either screwed in or snapped in. If no screws are visible, it is the later snap in type. Just give it a rap with a rubber mallet or yank with your hand.

Coupe Headliner Removal

Now, do you need to remove the headliner? If torn or heavily stained (they were called cigar lighters), you do.

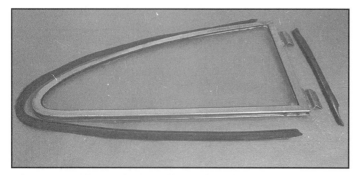

The outer rubber seal just pulls out from frame

Also it is tough to protect the headliner when painting the car and they are not that expensive. When removing, note the position of the clips that secure the headliner to the window/door openings. Remove interior lights by pulling out carefully and pulling off of the wire connector. Pull or cut the headliner down. The metal headliner hoops can be pulled out of their sockets. Save or plan to replace the rubber hoop ends. Leave the hoops in the headliner or mark them for location as they may differ in length. Many areas under the headliner have a muslin-like material, which is glued to ease headliner gluing. Try to save this material when removing the headliner material from the pillars. Plan to replace it if removed. Similar material can be found at fabric stores.

The sunroof headliner is similar, but there are no hoops and the sliding panel must be removed. This may be held by two small screws in the front. With the sliding panel and sunroof pushed back, you can remove the aluminum side rails and then pull out the sliding panel. On electric sunroof cars there is a metal brace that forms the curve of the sliding panel. It can be pulled back and off to make the sliding panel more flexible to aid in removal. Leave the headliner on the sliding panel.

Carpet

Carpet is next, and we are almost down to a naked 356. At the door opening, the carpet is held down by an aluminum strip. Remove it. The carpet will pull off as it was glued. You will find carpet nails in some locations. Try to save them and mark their locations. Below the rear seats, there are two chrome luggage strap brackets that have to be removed. Clean the threads of the screws behind the carpet on the vertical panel and use penetrating oil as these are often difficult to remove. The brackets should be pointing up.

The next parts that are very difficult to remove are the seat rails on the tunnel. On early 356s, the carpet is under the rails. If it ever got wet, the seat rail screws probably rusted solid to the weld nuts in the tunnel. Try your penetrating oil overnight. Cut away as much carpet as possible. With the proper size screwdriver, strike each screw head with a hammer. Try to tighten then loosen. Try not to damage the screw heads. If after many tries, they don't come loose you will have to drill out the screw heads. Remove the seat rail and try vise grips, heat and whatever on the remaining screw threads. Worse case is a screw will snap off flush and have to be drilled out and re-tapped. Now you know why some shops don't like to work on 356s. The outer seat rails are more easily removed by the nuts or allen head bolt.

On early models, there may be fresh air regulators located above the radio speaker area on both passenger and driver sides. These regulators have knobs and a rod that penetrate the carpet. The rod is an eccentric that has a flat side that grips in a tube to hold the fresh air vent in various positions or it could be a compression fitting. It is often frozen in the tube and will need penetrating oil. The fresh air regulator must be removed from the door jam side. There may be a chassis cavity under the regulator on the door jam side. Plug it with a rag so you don't drop parts into the chassis. Note the orientation of nuts and washers that secure the vent piece to the rod. Once they are removed, the rod, knob and bezel can be pulled away from the carpet.

Threshold

A threshold rubber seal is secured by a U shaped metal piece and four screws. There is usually rust in this area.

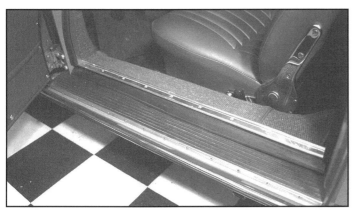

The threshold area. Note that the threshold rubber may have a wide rib that goes to the outside. It is held under the outside deco strip.

Lift up the rubber seal to get to the screws. You may have to sacrifice them. There is another aluminum strip securing the threshold rubber mat. This is secured with small screws that easily snap off. You can reach the screw tips under the threshold and brush them clean and hit with penetrating oil. Tap each screw before removal. The threshold rubber is glued down and should pull off. A cross section view of this area is shown on page 128 of *Authenticity*.

Interior Panels

Now for the interior panels. On coupes, the rear panel comes off first. The chrome luggage strap bracket, which points up, is secured by screws that either have nuts on the fire wall of the engine compartment or are secured to a bracket with weld nuts. With the strap brackets off, the rear panel is secured by multiple long posts that go

On later 356s the chrome luggage strap brackets are secured by weld nuts. On this panel holes were cut for rear speakers.

through the firewall with washers and clip nuts pushed on inside the engine compartment. You can work the Tinnerman nut off with pliers. They will probably have to be replaced. When installed at the factory, the rear panel had longer posts, which were cut short after installation. Leave all insulation behind panels in place unless it is in an area that will need repair. One area where insulation may need to be removed is under the quarter windows. Often rain coming in an open quarter window behind the side panel would cause rust on the inner fender panel.

The top of the side panel is called a garnish rail and is secured by a screw below the location of the quarter win-

The tab that supports the rear garnish rail on a T6 coupe. The tab on earlier cars was longer.

19

dow hinge screws and the tab that goes alongside the back panel. Remove the side panel garnish rail and there may be a clip securing the side panel to the bracket that the top piece sits on. The side panel may be glued on. If so, use a putty knife to work the material off. If you have the one- or two-piece seat back, they are secured by outboard chrome plated screws into the chassis. You probably removed them to get to that section of the carpet. Seat bottoms are glued in but can be worked out.

Rear Axle Nuts

Before removing the pedal cluster, it can be used along with the engine weight to make loosening of the rear axle nuts easier. You will need a 36 mm or 1 7/16 (cheaper) socket. A pipe wrench won't work. Remove the cotter pin that goes through the nut/axle. With the emergency brake on and someone holding down the brake pedal, attach an extension to a three-quarter inch breaker bar on the socket and leverage loose the axle nut. Both axle nuts unscrew counter clockwise. The easier way to do this is to borrow or rent an impact wrench and special hardened socket. This air-driven tool both hammers and twists on the nut. With the nut loosened, secure it finger tight and reinsert the cotter pin.

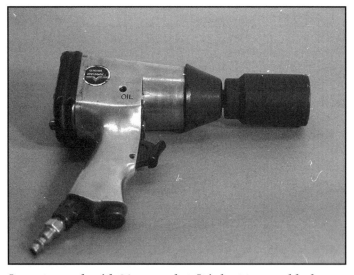

Impact wrench with 36 mm socket. It is best to use a black hardened socket with an impact wrench.

Remaining Interior Parts

All that is left is the shifter, heat control, accelerator pedal, pedal boards and the pedal cluster. You will have to remove the heater control wires where they attach to the flapper boxes under the engine. The shifter is removed by three bolts and a special oval washer, and on the later 356s, pulls right out. On earlier 356s, you will have to remove a pin that connects the shifter to the tunnel shift rod. The heater control is removed by bolts and then pulled forward with the wires that runs through the tunnel in tubes to the engine. The wires will come out greasy so use some rags to clean them as they are pulled out. The accelerator pedal is removed by two bolts. The pedal boards may be

The pedal cluster. The pivot piece is mounted vertically on the tunnel and is where the throttle rod connects.

secured by a clip at the top and the accelerator stop bolt on the driver's side and bolt and washer on the passenger's side. They will lift out with perhaps a little prying back of the bottom toe board mount. On real early 356s with square pedals, the pedal cluster is welded to the floor pan and you will either have to cut it out or work around it, depending on floor pan repair required. On all other 356s, you need to remove the two bolts that secure the master cylinder to the pedal cluster and then the three nuts that secure the pedal cluster to the floor. The clutch cable attachment to the pedal cluster will need some cleaning and penetrating oil for removal. You can put a small long nose vise grip on the solid cable end to keep it from spinning and push to get slack. With the pedal cluster removed, you can remove the pivot piece for the accelerator rod. This piece will need cleaning and lubrication before reinstallation. The hand throttle, if present, connects to this piece.

Exterior Parts

All the fasteners for the exterior parts are under the 356 and have been exposed to the elements. Spend some time and clean out these fasteners and hit them with penetrating oil. Give it time to work. Removal of most all the exterior parts is obvious; here are details for those areas that can give problems.

Headlights are easy. They are secured by one screw with a plastic or metal collar at the bottom of the headlight. The screw goes into a weld nut on the chassis. If it is missing, make a note to repair this prior to paint. With the screw out, the headlight pulls out and the three wire socket can be pulled off the headlight bulb.

The bolts securing the upper horn grilles on later 356s can snap off. If this happens or happened in the past, make a note to drill and tap this area. You will need a right angle drill attachment or removal of the fender bracket to make this repair. It is difficult to repair once the car is painted.

The front turn signal on 1960-65 356s have long threaded studs. Because of the body curve, one of the studs will have lots of threads exposed and the nut will be tight to the backing piece and difficult to remove. Take your time here.

The beltline side trim on open 356s (first used on Speedsters and optional on other models) is held on by snaps and a few T-bolts. The T-bolts are usually at the ends. You want to remove this carefully. If it can be restored, you not only save money, but time. The reproduction decos are manufactured differently than the originals and require modification to install. Find the T-bolt nuts and remove them. The deco can then be snapped off by inserting a craft stick (like a Popsicle stick) under the deco and prying up. Save the T-bolts and snaps. The snaps have been compressed and may or may not be reusable, but new ones are available from vendors.

Scripts on the 356 were secured by fasteners that were welded behind the panel. Prying the script off will damage this fastener and it may not be reusable. New scripts come with new fasteners but they are difficult to install. This will be covered later. Except for the first couple of years, Coachbuilder badges are riveted and you will have to grind the peened end to remove. Often they have been replaced and secured with screws.

On 356s with teardrop taillights, there is a rubber plug inside the engine compartment that when removed will allow you to get a socket on the innermost nut. With this loosened and the two outer nuts removed, the taillight will slide outward and come off. There will be an oval backing plate behind the taillight unit. Note its orientation.

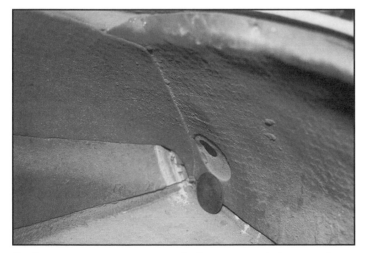

Engine compartment access to the inner nut securing tear drop taillight.

Hood Hinges

In the front compartment, there is a 14 ATF bolt above the hinge pocket that secures the hinge. Note its orientation. On later 356s, a relay may have to be removed to access the bolt. There is another bolt at the top of the hinge pock-

et under the dash. With these bolts removed, the hinge will pull out. Put the bolts back on the hinge in the same orientation.

Hood Hinge Repair

If the hinge was hanging up when you did a check prior to disassembly, it should be repaired now. You will be using the hood as a jig for repairs and will need it to open and close easily. Since rear lid hinges don't wear as much as front hood hinges, you can use one that works well as an example while performing the following procedures on the hood hinge. Hold the hinge with the star wheel pointing up. With your thumb and forefinger on the bolt on the pawl (the piece that moves the star wheel), push the pawl toward the star wheel. Use some force as you are simulating the weight of the hood. The star wheel should move a third of the way around. It probably won't move since it needs repair, but this is the testing procedure and it will be necessary to keep making little repairs until the star wheel goes around at least a dozen times without hang ups.

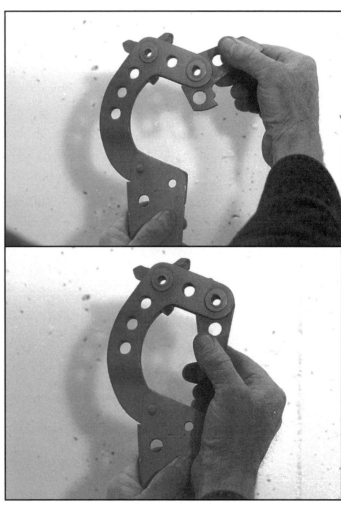

Testing the hood hinge

The first step is to see if the gap between the two sides of the hinge is equal. If not, place steel rulers or other metal in the gap and hammer or press in a vise to an equal gap. The star wheel should spin easily. The second step is to file off the burrs on the side of the star wheel and pawl. Test again. Note what is happening. See how the pawl pulls down and pushes up the star wheel. What a piece of engineering! The pointed part of the star wheel should be flat with a slight rounding at the tip and the part of the pawl that pulls it down should also be flat. Use a file to get these areas flat but take no more than four to six passes with the file. Test again. Can you see what is supposed to be happening? If it's not happening and you think it should, use a little file work and test. Maybe one star wheel position works. Great! This will be your model to get the others to look and work the same. Repeat minimal filing and testing until you can cycle it a dozen times. There is no need to use the grinder or add metal by welding. While this repair is tough to describe, it is not that hard to visualize during repair. There is an illustration of the hood hinge on page 28 of the *Restoration Guide*. Some repairs take little time, some longer. When you get it done, congratulate yourself. You also saved hundreds of dollars.

If the center tunnel does not need to be replaced, leave the wiring harness in the 356. You will probably not have to repair the wiring harness. It may have been modified by a previous owner, but it is nothing you can't fix, plus you should have some level of comfort from the electrical check you did prior to disassembly.

Leave the suspension as is for the time being. All the grease and dirt on the suspension will protect it during media blasting and painting. You can detail the suspension after paint.

Horns

Removal of the horn is straightforward, but it helps to loosen the 17 mm nut so the horn can be rotated to reach the wire connection. Use penetrating oil and a long screwdriver to remove the wire connection screws.

Engine Removal

There are different approaches to engine removal. They all must have worked, but some are safer than others. The following procedure has worked safely for dozens of engine removals. First, slide a heavy piece of plastic or cardboard under the engine on the floor. Jack up the 356 under the transmission hoop. Place jack stands under the axle tubes next to the heater cans, lower the 356. It does not have to be high in the air, just with the tires up a few inches.

Under the car, remove the gas line where it connects to the metal line behind the fan shroud. Be prepared for some fuel to drip; do not have a light nearby. Disconnect the tachometer cable (if present) at the rear of the engine. Disconnect the paper heater hoses. Disconnect the rods from the heater boxes to the heater cans.

From behind the engine shroud, pop off the linkage rod from the transmission bell crank; remove the linkage pull rod. Remove the two lower nuts securing the engine to the

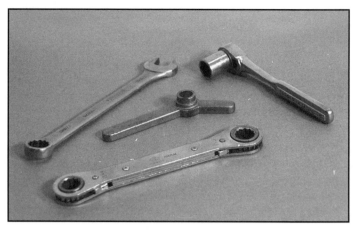

17 mm tools for engine nut/bolt removal. The magnet one is in the middle.

transmission. Now, support the engine with a floor jack. Use a piece of carpet on the jack cup to prevent damage to the sump plate. Have a helper under the car reach up and find the bolt head up by where the gas line and linkage rod go into the engine compartment. Have the helper secure it with a 17 mm wrench or socket. Reach behind the fan shroud to find the nut in the same area. Remove the nut. A 17 mm ratcheting wrench is a great tool for this job. The last nut is the tricky one. Have your helper lie on his left side and reach over the transmission to find the remaining bolt head. This is a long bolt and nut that secures the starter to the engine. Once the bolt is found, secure with 17 mm wrench. There also is a special 17 mm magnetic wrench for this application (available from 356 Registry vendors). *We found one still attached to the bolt after many miles.* Find the nut behind the fan shroud and remove it. This gets easier the more times you do it.

Remove the air cleaners and cover the carburetor with duct tape. (you don't want anything to fall into the engine.) Remove the rear most piece of horizontal engine sheet metal by removing the carburetor pre-heat air duct tubes and cross shaft first, if present.

Disconnect wires going to coil, oil pressure and oil temperature senders. Disconnect wires on generator. Raise the engine a little bit on the jack. Grab the fan shroud and muffler, wiggle the engine free. Pull the engine back until it clears the transmission. Now you have to raise the engine, tilting it forward until the horns on the heat exchanges clear the axle. When they do, you can lower the engine. Find some 4 x 4 and 2 x 4 wood so you can make a stand for both sides of the engine to allow removal of the jack. Jack up one side of the 356, using a safe jack point depending on the condition of the chassis. Lower the engine to your plastic or cardboard sheet by carefully removing the wood pieces. Slide the engine out. As long as the car is up in the air, now would be the time to remove the heater cans attached to the chassis. They may be rusted tight but will come off with penetrating oil and some gentle prying at the seams. The heater cans are primarily mufflers to keep noise out of the interior when the heater is not in use.

Chapter 3

Paint and Rust Removal

Required Tools

Tools used in this chapter include those used in the previous chapter, plus inexpensive wood chisels and wire brushes.

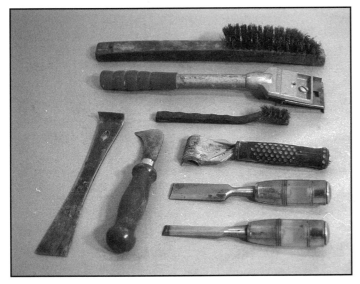

Additional tools needed are primarily for undercoat removal.

Basics

The paint on a 356 can be removed manually by sanding and/or paint removal chemicals. This method is very labor intensive and messy and doesn't remove rust. *The one time a customer didn't want to pay for blasting and we did this, we almost killed ourselves on the fumes and did not get the best welds.*

Sand blasting will remove paint and rust but works best on thick sheet metal. Thin sheet metal on the 356 can be warped by the heat generated by sand blasting.

Chemical dipping has advanced from its early days and can be used on 356s where many of the cavities have rusted and won't trap chemicals that can later leach out and

damage painted surfaces. The key to using this method is to find a company familiar with 356s.

The paint and rust removal process we recommend is media blasting. The media blasting process was developed by the Air Force to remove paint from aircraft without using chemicals. If you have to dip or blast or whatever, thoroughly investigate the process and any warranties. You will have to remove the wiring harness if you dip and take the suspension and gearbox out.

You can find media blasting shops and dippers under paint removal in the phone book. It would be wise to make an appointment and visit the shop and review their

Media blasting a 356. The worker is well protected and has a separate air supply. The media on the floor is reused until it's dust.

process. Ask what prep work you can do to reduce their prep time and your cost. In high humidity areas they may treat the metal with a product to reduce surface rust. Find out how to remove it prior to metal work. Ask about cost; they will probably give you a range as this is a time dependent process which varies due to paint hardness, procedures to be used and what is discovered.

If you take your disassembled 356 to a media blasting shop, you have more work to do.

Undercoat Removal

Blasting will usually remove most of the undercoat the Porsche factory provided. It will not remove the heavy undercoat put on by the previous owner in the 70s. This heavy undercoat has to come off as clean metal is needed to do metal repair. If the undercoat appears loose and flaky, you could have the blaster remove as much as possible and then do the rest yourself by hand, or you can remove the undercoat prior to blasting and the blaster can then give you a really clean surface.

To remove the undercoat there is no magic. Others have reported using dry ice, WD-40, chemicals, heat, air chisels and other procedures. What works for us is a selection of various size inexpensive wood chisels and wire brushes. The chisels can be sharpened as needed. A curved carpet knife helps to get in crevasses. The process is straightforward; just wear eye protection, gloves and old clothes. You don't need to clean the suspension. It will be done later.

After the undercoat is removed, protect those areas you don't want blasted. All the exposed wires under the car, in the front and rear compartments and behind the dash (if you are having it blasted) need to be protected. First wrap the wires in aluminum foil, then cover with duct tape. The blast shop will probably put their own heavy duty duct tape over yours, but you have identified the wires you want protected. The reason for the aluminum foil is that tape applied directly to wires for a long time is difficult to remove and leaves residue. The aluminum foil protects the wire from this.

You will want to cover the emergency brake tube since you don't want blasting media in there. Also cover both ends of the fuel line in the tunnel. You should cover the vent on top of the transmission and the input shaft area of the transmission. It is best to leave the shocks on the 356 for transport. They can be protected with foil and duct tape. One area that is hard to protect (but you can try) is the heating tubes in the longitudinals.

We always enjoy the phone call, "Jim, we have been driving our restored 356 and we used the heater for the first time. We have media dust all over the interior." We have made special attachments for the vacuum cleaner and air hose, but this dust appears to be a "thank you" from the 356.

Before taking the chassis, doors, lids and bumpers to the blaster, write up exactly what you want done. You want all paint, bondo and rust removed. They will use the media process on the paint and a sand process on the bondo and rust. They don't have to blast the floor if you are going to replace it; just have them do the edges. They don't have to blast the wheels, brake drums or suspension areas; this can be done later. You may not need to have the insides of the

doors blasted, but you should have them blast the inner lower seam. So write up what you want done and go over it with them. They may provide some additional ideas as they have blasted many vehicles. If you have a piece such as a door hinge plate cover, rear deck lid or T6 gas filler lid that has the original paint color that you want to match, save it for a paint match and hand strip it or have it media blasted later.

To transport your 356 to the blaster or dipper, it is probably best to use a trailer, whether you borrow, rent or use your own. Flat tow devices usually attach to the front bumper brackets and these may not be solid before and/or after blasting. If you have never loaded or trailered a 356, get advice from someone that has or use a tow service. Safe tie down points on a 356 are not obvious. Use the front lower A arms and rear transmission hoop with secondary chains around the axle tubes.

The come-alongs are secure to straps around the control arms.

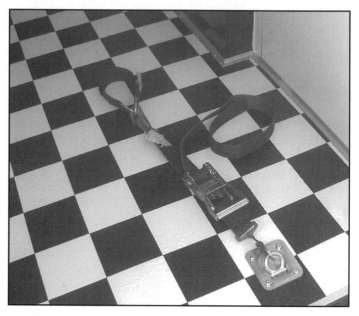

Ratcheting tie down and axle strap can be used to secure the rear on each side.

24

Seat Disassembly

The seats were some of the first items removed when the 356 was disassembled. While the car is at the blast shop or dipper, now would be a good time to check them. The condition of the material will determine what should be done. If springs are not poking through and they feel comfortable, you may want to just cover them with a seat cover and use them for awhile. If the material is torn or worn, you will probably want to have them reupholstered. This is not a do-it-yourself project. Special tools and jigs are needed to ensure seats are correct.

If you find an auto upholstery shop in your area, make sure they have done 356 seats and know where to get proper materials. Vendors of upholstery materials and capable shops are listed on the 356 Registry web site. When the seat bottoms are assembled it is important that they get the *smile*; this is the crease across the seat that provides a good fit and is distinctive to the 356. If you have your Certificate of Authenticity (or Kardex info), it may tell if the original seats were leather. This and cost will determine if you go with leather seats.

The seats are disassembled by first removing the three chrome screws on the vertical sides of the hinges. Be careful; the screws go into weld nuts on the interior of the frame. If you break one, the upholstery will have to be removed to make a repair (there is a repair shown on page 239 in the *Restoration Guide*). With the side screws removed, the seat back can be removed. The chrome screw at the hinge pivot point can be removed to remove the hinge. Note the presence, size and number of any fiber washers (spacers). There is also a special serrated cup washer under the screw. With the hinge removed, the seat bottoms and backs can be taken or sent to the upholstery shop. If you are going to have a complete interior installed, the seats can be stored until after the car is painted. Upholstery work is done after paint. If you decide to re-chrome your seat hinges, take pictures and detailed drawings during disassembly. Some seat hinges have a cover with a peened stud that has to be drilled for

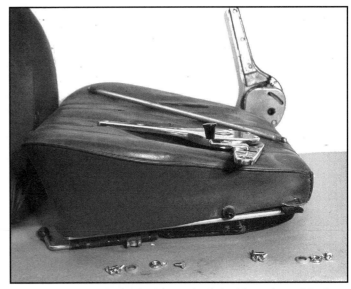

Note that there are plastic spacers both inside and outside the hinge pivot. Spacers differ in type and number.

removal. The stud can be tapped for a machine screw for reassembly.

Long Lead Time Items

Certain items always require advance planning due to long lead times. Two of these are keys and chrome.

Keys

During your pre-restoration inspection, you noted what keys you had and which worked. On the 356 Registry web site is contact information for a vendor that specializes in 356 keys. Contact him for advice on your key needs. There will be key codes on the locks that he will need to know. He can tell you how to find them.

If you have to disassemble a door handle for chroming, the later ones are easiest. They just have a circlip that pries off. Earlier assemblies have a small screw and perhaps a metal wedge that has to be driven out. The transmission lock in the shifter has a small screw. As usual, note the orientation of all parts during disassembly.

Chrome

Now would be a good time to evaluate and decide what to do with the chrome plated pieces you boxed separately during disassembly. Some pieces may just need buffing to restore their luster. This could be done at a plating shop, antique restoration shop or even a jeweler. A local jeweler did a great job on a Roadster windshield side post that had been chromed, but then scratched during bodywork. Buffing, also called coloring is not that expensive.

Some parts may need to be re-chromed or replaced, particularly if pitted. Originality is an issue. If you know, for example, that your hood handle is original to your 356 you may want to re-chrome it. Reproduction hood handles are

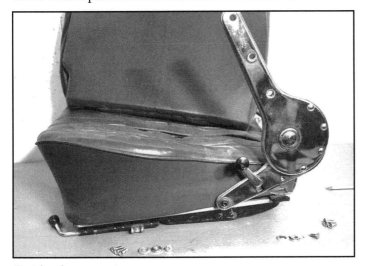

Seat hardware

available, you might simply want to replace it. It is funny, but the cost to re-chrome is often close to or more than the cost to replace.

If you decide to re-chrome, selecting a chrome shop is very important. We have used three different shops in the Denver area. One took way too long, one lost some important small parts and the shop we use now has inconvenient business hours but cost, quality and schedule are all good. All the shops charged about the same for similar parts. When we have had all the chrome done on a 356, it cost between $1,000 and $1,500 depending on the model.

If there isn't a local chrome shop in your area, it will be necessary to send parts out. We used a shop on the East Coast that could re-chrome aluminum (which the local shop could not). Their process was to photograph all the parts received and then return photos along with a contract outlining their terms, conditions, prices and schedule. This is a comfortable and secure way of doing business. The price for re-chroming at the East Coast shop was almost exactly the same as the local shop for the same part.

We decided to re-chrome all the parts on a really nice 1961 Roadster. When we took them to the local shop, he said, "can't do these; they're aluminum." The two parts were the rear bumper guards with the exhaust hole. The head pieces for these rear bumper guards were pot metal, which the local shop could re-chrome. We had to send the rear bumper guards to the East Coast shop, but the question was why were they aluminum? Carreras had aluminum bumper guards, but they didn't have exhaust holes. A little research did not uncover definitive answers. Another of those 356 mysteries.

The chroming process involves preparing the part by cleaning and then protecting threaded areas. The part is then de-chromed or reverse plated using a sulfuric acid solution. Rust is blasted and any metal repairs made. Layers of copper are built up, buffed until a smooth surface is achieved and then a layer of nickel and finally a very thin layer of chrome is applied. This is called triple plating. Triple plating does not mean three layers of chrome. The part is then buffed or colored. Buffing is an acquired skill as the chrome layer is thin and very easy to burn through.

Parts which are only nickel plated, are the pre-1962 seat rails. Let the chrome shop know it is not to be chrome-plated. You will also have to drill out the rivets to remove the springs prior to plating. Note that the rivet has been peened over a lip on the rivet hole. Drill only a little way to preserve this lip; then use a smaller bit to drill out the rivet. Replacement rivets and seat rail springs are available from vendors.

When you receive your re-chromed parts, you should use your tap and die set to de-burr all threaded areas. If you don't do this, you will have assembly problems. When you reassemble a re-chromed seat hinge you will have to file all areas that fit into each other. The hardest part of seat hinge assembly is the main spring. You will have to secure the assembly to your workbench and make a tool to move the spring end to its notch. We welded a pin to a bearing race and attached a long handle. (There is also a tool shown in the *Restoration Guide*.)

The first time we reassembled a seat hinge, we put the spring in backwards. All seemed fine as the catch held the seat in an upright position. At a club driving event, the instructor drove the 356 to show us the track and the race line. After a few laps, he pulled in and we switched positions. As we were cleared onto the track, the instructor went to adjust his seat and was thrown backwards! We were through turn five before he got upright.

Door Window Frame

Another part that is tricky to disassemble and reassemble is the door window frame with the vent window. The non-vent window frame is all one piece with just the air deflector piece at the rear to be removed. The four small screws may or may not need to be re-chromed. The early (through 1961) vent window frame may require removal of the rivet piece at the vent window hinge. The later (1962-65) vent window hinge uses a pin but is still tricky to disassemble. The first step is to remove the vent window section from the frame. This section is secured by two sets of two long, small-diameter screws and a short screw secured to a

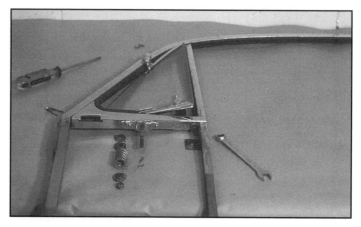

Preparing to drill out the seat rail spring. One is shown on the left. Two drill bits are used to preserve the lip into which the rivet is peened.

Window frame hardware

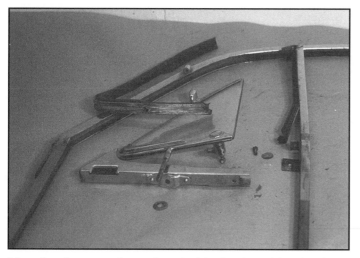

Note that there may be washers inside the riveted bracket for the pivot stud. In this case, there was one washer.

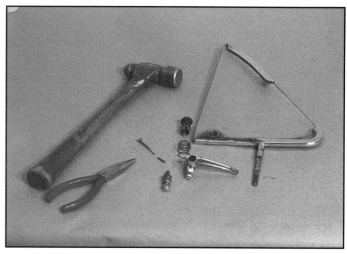

There were five thin wave washers on this vent window locking mechanism.

bracket by the locking mechanism.They are prone to breaking. To get penetrating oil to them you will have to partially remove the vent window rubber seal. To do this, open the vent window and pull out the rubber seal. It will still be attached at the bottom, but you can see where to spray the penetrating oil. Remove the four long screws and the short screw that is hiding under the bottom rubber. The vent window assembly can now be removed from the frame.

At the bottom of the vent window is a pivot stud with a spring and special washers and a nut. Note the location of the hardware prior to disassembly. The pivot stud is also prone to breaking so use penetrating oil and proceed with caution. There is a flat side on the pivot stud to secure locking pliers while removing the nut.

For the early vent window with rivets, the chrome piece that holds the hinge to the glass must be removed. This can be done with a X-acto Knife and blade. Keep working it between the piece and the glass until it separates. Now the vent window and lower rubber can be removed. Disassembly of the locking mechanism will require good notes for future reassembly. First, the pin has to be tapped out. Then carefully disassemble the mechanism, noting the number and location of the very thin wave washers. Now the lower part of the vent window can also be worked free with the X-acto Knife.

Hardware

Also while you wait for the blaster, you can make a decision on hardware. So far, we have left most of the hardware on the removed parts and spent some quality time in the evening with metric tap and die set. Some hardware will be damaged and needs to be replaced. Trim hardware should be replaced; kits are available. Plan to clean the hardware with the rotary wire brush on your bench

grinder as you install the parts. Since most of the hardware will be painted or undercoated by the time the car is finished, this will be sufficient.

Do not reuse damaged hardware. There are specialty shops you can find in the phone book that sell metric hardware. Also some large hardware centers sell metric hardware. As mentioned earlier, 14 mm ATF bolts are no longer available. Try to restore this hardware.

An alternative is to remove all the hardware from your parts and have them cleaned and plated. This will involve extensive notes of which hardware goes with which part. Plating involves soaking the hardware in muriatic acid with a water rinse and neutralizing with a baking soda solution. Then the hardware is tumbled in a rock tumbler or something similar. Then the hardware is cad or zinc plated. Both approaches will work. It is your call.

Coal or Candy

It's like Christmas! The blast shop calls and says your 356 is ready to be picked up. What was hiding under all the old paint and undercoat? You may find previous repairs done with brazing. You may find sloppy welding repairs with pinholes. You may find a piece of rebar welded or brazed under the hood where it was kinked. Hopefully, you will find that just typical rust repairs are needed.

The following is a story that grabbed me; maybe it will grab you. We were evaluating a '65 C Coupe. It was a family 356, purchased new by the owner's father. Basically, we were evaluating the 356 to inform the owner how he could stay ahead of problems and make the car look better. It was old and tired. The owner knew the history of the 356 from day one. When I noticed a small area of damage, he commented he didn't know how it happened as he was missing in action for awhile. It hit me. I said, "Hanoi, Hilton?" He said, "yes, about six years." I stuck out my hand and said, "Thanks for coming back."

Chapter 4

Metal Work

There are a number of options on metal work. With the car disassembled and media blasted or dipped, all the damaged metal can be seen. A body shop experienced with the 356 Porsche should be able to give you an estimate for repairs. The problem often is finding a body shop with 356 experience in your area. Perhaps, a shop experienced with Volkswagens will do the work; but to get a reasonable estimate, you will have to provide them a catalog with prices and descriptions of 356 metal repair parts.

Another option might be to find an experienced body man to do the work on his own time. You would provide all the repair pieces as needed and also do some of the grunt work like grinding.

You can also do it yourself. If you don't have automotive repair skills, you could take a vo-tech class in automotive repair, but those classes mostly cover panel replacement on newer cars; the 356 has few replacement panels. A class on welding will help but may cover more than just automotive welding.

You could learn how to do welding yourself. Acquire the necessary tools, buy some car hoods from a junk yard, have them media blasted and cut them up and weld them back together. You might even be able to find someone to coach you as you learn the skills.

Doing it yourself is certainly the most cost effective way and the most rewarding. The first issue is tools. The one reason our shop has been able to get so many 356s repaired and restored is the plasma cutter. This is a tool that takes air from a compressor (50 psi) and converts it to a plasma gas and with a positive and negative field cuts through metal like drawing with a pencil. No distortion, no rough edges, easy curve cuts; it is the perfect tool for removing damaged metal on a 356. They are 110 volts, fairly small in size and easily moved around. They will work with a portable air compressor. They are expensive - more expensive than a MIG welder.

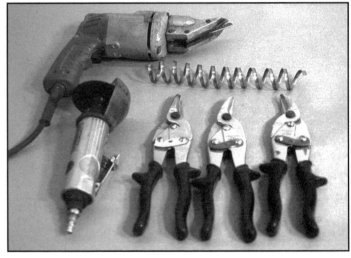

Metal cutting tools. The side cutter is on the left below the electric shear. Three aviation tins snips are shown for right, left and straight cuts. The curly piece is what the electric shear creates and is perfect for the shop Christmas tree.

In the early days, we used to make house calls. We could transport the air compressor, plasma cutter, MIG welder, some 20-gauge sheet metal and tools to the location of a 356 needing repair. On one such trip, we were at a garage and we asked the owner where the electrical outlets were. "Over there," he said. Sure enough. One two-plug outlet in the whole garage. We had extension cords going to the kitchen and dining room to get the job done.

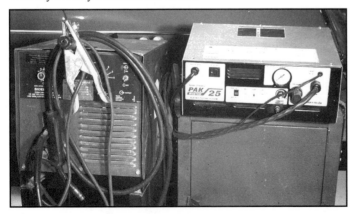

Plasma cutter on right; MIG welder on left

The alternative to a plasma cutter is a side cutter or die grinder with cut off wheel. The side cutter is an air-powered tool (90 psi) and will only cut straight lines. Other tools, like nibblers or saws, may distort the metal. The plasma cutter is the best bet with the side cutter a second choice.

It may be possible to rent a plasma cutter or join in with some friends and buy and share a plasma cutter. If you rent a plasma cutter, don't think you can cut out all the areas to be repaired and then return it. This is not the way it is done. You will start in one area, complete the repair and move on to the adjoining area. In addition to the plasma cutter, you will need a MIG welder with gas. There are inexpensive MIG welders without gas, but they will not work. Good MIG welders are available in 110 volts. The gas used is carbon dioxide (CO_2) or a CO_2/Argon mix. TIG welders are great but best used at a workbench. You need one hand to hold the torch, one hand to feed the weld source (wire) and one hand (usually a foot) to control the equipment. Hard to do, lying on your back working on a repair to a 356 battery box. Some TIG welders do have a hand control.

In addition to a plasma cutter and MIG welder, you'll need an air compressor to run the plasma cutter and various air tools. A small portable air compressor will drive the plasma cutter, but it will have difficulty keeping a side cutter or die grinder at speed. But a bigger air compressor is better, five horsepower minimum.

In addition to the three main tools - plasma cutter, MIG welder and air compressor - you will need the following:

Tools
- An electric shear and aviation tin snips
- Side cutter (air) w/ 3" cut off wheel
- Die grinder (air) w/ 3/16" grinding wheel (3M part #4292)
- Rotary tool (Dremel) w/ various metal grinding stones
- Right angle grinder w/ 4.5" grinding wheels
- Metal punch (air)
- Spray gun
- Various size C clamps
- Propane torch
- Undercoat gun
- Inexpensive 500 watt shop light

Grinding tools. Two angle grinders, one with wire brush, one with grinding wheel. The die grinder is in the center and a rotary tool to its right.

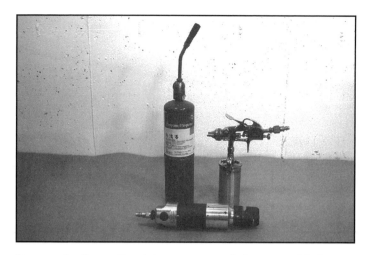

Propane torch, small paint spray gun and air powered hole punch/flanging tool.

Another valuable tool to have is a stud welder. This is an electric tool that welds metal studs to a panel. You can then use a puller or slide hammer to move metal. In the old days they would drill holes and use a slide hammer with a hook. You may see those holes on your 356. Stud welders used to be expensive but are now down to around $150.

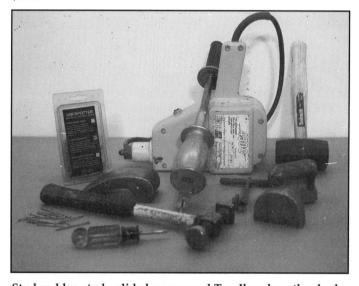

Stud welder, studs, slide hammer and T puller plus other body working tools

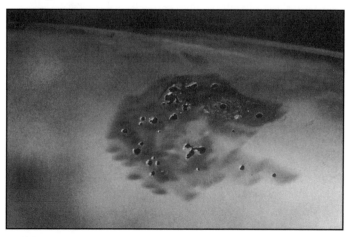

Pull holes that were just bondoed over with resultant rust

You also need the usual collection of shop tools: hammers, pliers, screwdrivers, drifts, chisels, etc. A source for inexpensive tools is Harbor Freight – harborfreight.com. While most of their tools are made overseas, they are functional. They also have stores in major cities that have excellent sales. Their normal price for car dollies, which we use to roll around 356s and engines, was $79 a pair, then $49 a pair on sale and then $39 a pair at a store sale. We buy most of our consumables at Harbor Freight i.e. grinding wheels and cut off wheels. We also buy small flux brushes in volume and use them for glue work. They are cheap enough to throw away after use. Another tool we buy in volume are craft sticks (popsicle sticks and/or tongue depressors). They are about $2 for 500. We use them to initially mix fillers, mix two-part cements and to push in rubber profiles/seals.

Welding Helmet

When I first started welding, I had a difficult time seeing the work area through the welding helmet even with a 500-watt light. I was using a number ten dark glass in my helmet. When I switched to number eight, my welding improved significantly. Most of the welding done on the 356 is using the lower power settings. While it is best to use the highest power setting that will do the work, often welding is done near thin metal and to avoid blowing it away it is necessary to use a lower setting.

Ear, eye, hand and respirator protection.

While we have only had one injury in 10 years, we did have two fires. One was when a rag with solvent was left in a 356 in the morning and in the afternoon some welding was being done and a spark ignited the rag. I saw the flames, which were three feet high, through the welding helmet and was able to grab the rags with my welding gloves and pitch them into a pail of water. The other fire was in a trash can under the workbench by a vise. We were using the vise for welding and a spark ignited some paper towels that had been used with solvent. The trash can was tipped over and the fire smothered. The trash can was relocated from under the vise and all rags and paper towels used with solvent are now taken outside the work area and stored in a fireproof container.

Rotisserie?

A rotisserie is a device that will put the 356 up off the ground and allow you to work on almost all areas standing up. There are various designs. You can purchase one, have one made or make one yourself. There are examples of rotisseries in the *Restoration Guide* (page 383).

While the rotisserie allows easy access to almost all areas, particularly the underneath of a 356, it does take room. Some restorers are concerned that the rotisserie puts undo stress on the chassis leading to misaligned repairs. They

Self-darkening helmet on the right, standard helmet on left, plus 500-watt halogen work light (under $15).

B.J. purchased one of the self-darkening helmets. They used to be quite expensive but now are affordable. I tried B.J.'s and it is great and I will get one when I need a new helmet. Get the opinion of a welding helmet supplier on what type of dark glass to use with your equipment.

Safety Equipment

In addition you need safety equipment: eye protection, ear protection, dust masks, respirator, gloves, 8# ABC fire extinguisher and a first aid kit. Don't go cheap on safety equipment. It is available at reasonable cost considering what can happen without it.

This rotisserie has side bars that make it stable, but the center pivot should be higher to ease rotation

This 356 really needed a rotisserie

Car dollies also can be used to move 356 engines and transmissions

prefer to work on a 356 supported at the suspension points. Other restorers use a rotisserie 100 percent of the time.

We used a rotisserie all the time in the early years of the shop. Later we seldom used it. As our experience grew, we were able to make bottom repairs quickly and it was easier to make other repairs, particularly around the doors, with the 356 on platforms and jack stands.

The issue may be one of time. If you expect to spend a lot of time on bottom repairs, a rotisserie may be for you. If you hope to proceed quickly and have few bottom repairs, you may not need one.

The joy of welding upside down. A case for a rotisserie.

Car Dolly

If you have space limitations or need to move your 356 around during restoration, a car dolly may be appropriate. Examples are shown on pages 391 and 394 of the *Restoration Guide*. When doing metal repair on your 356, do not use the dolly. Use the rotisserie or jack stands.

Sheet Metal

In addition to tools, you will also need sheet metal. You can purchase 4 x 8 sheets of 20-gauge sheet steel at most steel supply facilities or 4 x 4 sheets at most body shop supply houses. The 356 Porsche used 19-gauge sheet metal in most areas, but it is no longer available. Some areas of the 356 used lighter gauge metal and some heavier. There are places to use heavier 18-gauge metal, which will be discussed.

The 4 x 8 sheet of 20-gauge metal is only about $30, but if you need to have it cut to fit in your vehicle they may apply a shearing charge, so call ahead and ask. You can cut the full sheet in half with an electric shear or with tin snips for easier storage.

Welding Techniques

The most important welding technique is *clean, shiny metal!* As in many tasks, preparation is 80 percent of the job. You cannot weld to rust, brazing, lead, body filler or undercoating. Both sides of the repair area must be free of contaminates. The media blasting has not only revealed where the metal has been damaged but also where any brazing is that has to be removed. Brazing is done with a non-ferrous filler rod and low heat. It was popular because it caused little distortion and it was widely used by novices in the 50s and 60s. In fact, the factory actually did some brazing on your 356. Look for the factory brazing; it is that gold colored metal. Hint; look around the dash defroster vents.

The factory used lead to fit the doors and lids to specification. They also used it to smooth the contours, more in the early years and less as stampings improved and production grew. Blasting does not remove lead. You can see the lead around the doors and lids. There can be rust under the lead. If you can see bubbles in the lead or can see rust damage behind the lead, the lead will have to be removed.

Removing Lead-*Important!*

If there are children that will be in your work area, please take precautions when removing lead. Young children whose brains are still developing can be poisoned by ingesting lead particles. This means you are going to have to thoroughly clean the work area where you removed the lead. You must not take clothes or shoes into an area where young children are present; take every precaution you can to see that young children are not exposed to lead! End of sermon.

Removing lead is done using a propane torch and wire brush in areas where lead is present. Do this until no lead flows. Then use a wire wheel on your right angle grinder to remove any residue. When you see sparks you are getting to steel. Then use a rotary tool with a grinding stone to remove any remaining flux or lead on the surface. When all you see is sparks, the lead is gone.

Repair Technique

With lead removed and clean, shiny metal in the work area, inspect the area to determine where the good metal remains. Blasting will have blown away the rust and left a hole, but there may still be rust damage around the periphery of the area. If you see small pits, this is where there was surface rust that was blasted out. Where there are no pits you have good metal. Use a marking pen to indicate the edges of the good metal. With the plasma cutter, cut along your marks. Then use your rotary tool to clean the edges and back from the edge about one-half inch on both sides of the opening. Next, place a piece of cardboard *(we use manila file folders)* behind the opening and trace around the opening. Cut out the cardboard pattern and lay it on your 20-gauge metal. Trace with a scratch awl or pencil and cut with tin snips. Place the cut piece in the opening and check for fit. You want from one-thirty-second to one-sixteenth of an inch gap all around. Secure the patch in the opening *(believe it or not, we use duct tape – we tried magnets once, but they got messy)*. The duct tape is only used long enough to tack in the piece. You are going to tack the piece where it is tightest in the opening, so place your duct tape outside these areas. The duct tape may flame or melt but can be removed with your gloved hand after a few tacks.

Welding

The MIG welder has a wire supply and a gas supply. With a ground connected to the work area when you pull the trigger, the wire touches the repair surface, an arc is created and the wire melts creating a weld pool. As this is happening, the gas is flowing around the wire and shielding the weld from oxidation. Welding is the process of moving your weld pool between two areas of metal, causing them to flow together.

A tack weld is only about a quarter inch long. Place a

number of these around the opening again at the tightest edges. Ensure the edges are flush. You do your tacks at the tight edge as the heat of the weld will cause the metal to expand and come together. You want to direct the tip of your welder at a slight angle so the MIG wire will hit the new metal piece first. This is called the angle of attack. You will learn to adjust this angle as you work on repairs with various orientations. After tacking, you run one inch welds around the repair alternating areas. This is called butt welding. You always start your weld on top of a previous weld to avoid pinholes. Once the repair piece is welded in place, you can see that the heat marks on the metal only extended about a half inch. This is the beauty of MIG welding as compared to oxyacetylene welding, which transfers more heat and requires subsequent reworking of the metal. An experienced oxyacetylene welder can do beautiful work; after all, this is what the factory used. But the MIG welder is today's tool and can be quickly learned by the novice.

The above is a general description of the repair process. There will be specifics for work on each panel. After welding is grinding. Again, there is a grinding technique. You can use a right angle grinder with 4 1/2" grinding wheel or a thick three sixteenth of an inch cut off disc on a die grinder. With the die grinder, you can use the edge of the disc to grind the weld without getting into the surrounding area. You want the tool to do the job. You don't bear down on the grinder. You move the grinder around so the metal doesn't get hot and warp. You do not want to see the metal glow red. Grinding is a tedious, noisy job. You may want to save up your grinding for a grinding party when your roommate is out of the house.

Grinding. Note the use of eye, ear and breathing protection plus long sleeves, gloves and adequate light.

After grinding, you have to inspect the weld. Place your 500-watt light behind the repair and look for pinholes. Fill them in and regrind until they are gone.

Another welding technique is the rosette or plug weld. This is used where you have overlapping panels, like the

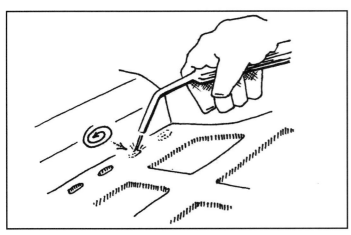

Plug welding – start at the inside edge of the hole and run your weld pool in decreasing circles until the hole is filled. Then lift your welding tip and release the trigger. The center of the weld will sag as it cools, simulating a spot weld.

floor pan to the inner longitudinal ledge. You punch or drill a hole *(Harbor Freight sells an air operated metal hole punch)*, clamp the pieces together and fill the hole with weld. This simulates a spot weld but will be stronger. A similar technique is hole filling. Say you have a hole, maybe a hole from a slide hammer repair. You can start your weld on the edge of the hole and work in circles until you fill it in. A trick is to secure a piece of aluminum or copper behind the hole to avoid cat whiskers. These are pieces of your MIG wire that didn't melt.

A welding technique similar to hole welding is what we call bridge welding. This is where you have a gap to fill, but it is wider than an eighth of an inch but too small to fit a repair piece. You can start at the edge of the gap and move your weld pool across the gap and then catch the edge of your bridge and fill in the area.

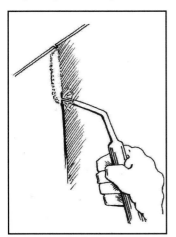 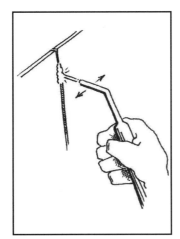

Tack weld – angle of attack. Aim over old metal to hit new metal

Bridge welding

Another technique we enjoy we call sculpting. This is where you have a vertical angled area to fill and you can start at the top and sculpt your weld pool to fill the area. All of these techniques are about moving your weld pool to create a repair. You will have to do this on the horizontal, vertical down, vertical up, around curves and upside

down. There is great satisfaction in doing a good weld in a difficult area. If you are not happy with any weld, cut it out and try again.

Doors and Hinges

Before starting the metal repairs on the 356, spend some time on the door hinges and hinge pins. Attaching and removing the door will be done numerous times to check fitting so this needs to occur effortlessly. First, check to see if your hinge pins are straight by rolling them on a flat surface. If not straight, it is best to get new ones rather than trying to make them straight. Then, fit the pin through the hinge on the lock post and door. With a small round file, work the hinges until the pin goes in easily, not tight. Don't even think about using a drill bit to speed up the process. A pin that is loose in the hinge will give you all sorts of problems.

Hang the door using the pins. Yes, the door may need repair but unless it is totally shot it will serve as a jig. You want the door to fit evenly in the opening. Getting it flush and the gaps perfect will be dealt with later. The door as a jig tells if the chassis is still in alignment as repairs are made. If you had to remove the hinge at the bolts, use four bolts and your shims to secure the hinge. They are all needed for proper positioning. Now with the doors on and centered, there is an additional step if you are working on an open car.

Bracing an Open 356

An open 356 will flex as the inner panels are removed and installed, so it is necessary to brace it. Bracing could be done at the door opening or even by welding the doors closed, but that would make it difficult to get in and out. It is best to get some long pieces of one inch square tubing at your metal supplier and weld them to the back bulkhead and the top of the dash. Check the doors to ensure they are still centered.

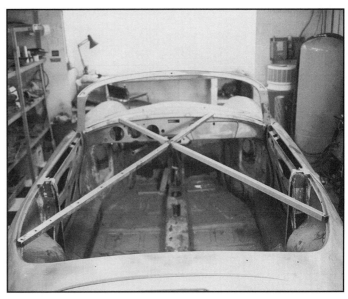

Floor pans will be removed on this 356 cabriolet so it is braced.

Supporting the 356

All this time the 356 may have been on its tires on the ground. Now is the time to remove the tires and get the 356 in the air.

We have wooden blocks that we use for a jack stand platform. It is two pieces of 2 x 12 lumber with plywood in the center. These were salvaged from wooden headers used in door and window construction. You can make something similar. With platforms for a jack stand, we can get a car two feet or more off the ground. The platforms with jack stands are a lot safer than jack stands alone.

Jack and jack stand placement at the front. Under the jack stand is a piece of thin plywood as this 356 did not sit evenly on the jack stand. These jack stands also have a notch that secures the front sway bar bracket without damage.

Place the stands at the outer end of the rear torsion tubes and under the front sway bar mounts. Your 356 may not fit flat on the jack stands. This is not uncommon and is probably due to 40 to 50 years of flexing. Just use plywood to shim the low jack stand so the 356 is equally supported on all four corners.

Evaluation

With the 356 off the ground, remove the doors and evaluate repairs to the tunnel, floor pan and inner ledges. Start with the rear floor pan. It goes under the tunnel and sits on ledges of the inner longitudinal and rear section. Rust damage can occur anywhere along this area. The simplest floor repair can be to just patch repair part of the floor pan without removing it. More extensive repair would be rebuilding the tunnel and ledge area and replacing the rear floor pan.

To make a patch repair, you will have to order a rear floor pan and cut out a patch. Why do this when you could replace the whole floor pan since you paid for it? Well, with this area blasted, you can see if the original factory seams and welds are intact. If they are, why disturb them?

They have lasted for 40 to 50 years. There is an excellent article on floor repair by Ron Roland in the *Restoration Guide* on pages 314-319. Ron is an excellent illustrator and his articles are very well written.

Rear Floor Pan

The floor pan you ordered may have been treated with a zinc galvanizing material. This will have to be removed along any edge that you weld. The galvanizing treatment, if not removed, will give off a harmful gas plus make a poor weld when heated. Remove it using the right angle grinder. To make the floor pan patch, cut along the top edges of the old floor pan depressions. Clean your edges

Rear floor pan that will be patched.

Floor pan section being cut out with a side cutter. Note proper use of safety equipment.

with the rotary tool. Then cut a similar section from the new floor pan but cut it a little larger. Place the new section under the cut out, using a small jack and wood, and mark and trim. Tack in place and weld; carefully grind your weld flush. A patch to the front floor pan would be done the same way.

Preparing the rear floor pan patch.

Tacking in the floor pan patch.

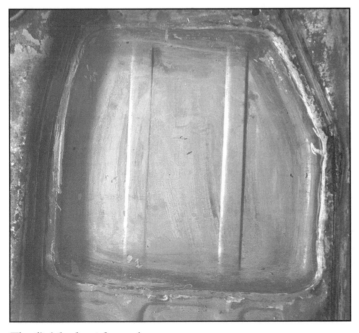
The finished patch repair.

For more extensive repair, cut out the floor pan, staying inside the ledge area, which is about an inch out. At the front of the rear floor pan is a groove that mates with an opposite groove on the front floor pan to make a transverse hollow tube for floor pan rigidity. If you are going to replace the front floor pan, cut in front of the tube. If you are only replacing the rear, cut behind the tube and leave it intact. You may or may not have to cut out the rear seat mounts depending on condition. If they are OK, you can cut around them leaving them attached to the sides. You

Rear floor pan removed and repairs to inner longitudinal and tunnel.

will have to remove the piece of the original floor pan underneath them. The floor pan will come out in two pieces (left and right) since the floor pan is still attached under the tunnel. On 356 and 356A, the floor pan is different in the area under the tunnel. One vendor has a reproduction floor pan with this difference; others may not. Ask. If this area is not damaged on the pre-1960 car, you may want to leave it and replace the rear floor pan in two pieces.

To remove the piece under the tunnel, don't use the plasma cutter since it could cut into the fuel line, brake line or wiring tube. Use the side cutter from underneath, only going in about a quarter inch. With the tunnel piece out, grind down all the metal from the floor pan that remains on the ledges. An alternative to this approach is to drill out all the spot welds securing the floor pan to the ledges. There are special spot weld drill bits for this application. Ask at the hardware store. You could also use the plasma cutter to blow out the spot welds. One advantage of media blasting is that it is fairly easy to see spot welds. Removing the spot welds will take more time than the cutting and grinding approach, but both techniques work.

With the pan out, begin by repairing the ledges. A perimeter kit is available from vendors. These are pieces of angled metal to repair the inner longitudinal and provide a ledge. You could make your own repair pieces if you have a sheet metal brake to make the angle. The pieces should be 4 1/8 inches tall with a three-fourths inch lip.

When we were starting out and before we got our own brake (in exchange for doing work on a Speedster), we called around and found a local sheet metal shop that cut and bent the pieces we needed.

The repair to the perimeter and ledges is done by cutting at the first bend of the inner longitudinal, which is 4 1/8 inches up from the floor pan. Rust damage seldom gets up this high. Cut out as much of the perimeter as needed, leaving any good areas. This will help you line up the repair area with the original metal. Repair one side at a time.

Tunnel repair is a little trickier because brackets and tubes are welded to the sides of the tunnel. With the floor pan off the tunnel, you can see what you have to work around. Repairs to the tunnel are similar to the perimeter; you just have to stay away from the tube holding the wiring harness.

With the perimeter and tunnel repairs completed, the rear floor pan can be installed. First, clean and paint the tunnel. There will be surface rust inside the tunnel. There are many options to deal with the surface rust. It can be painted with a rust neutralizer, painted with a special rust encapsulation paint or cleaned with acid and painted with a two-part epoxy paint.

Probably the best application for this area would be a product like POR-15. This is a special paint that dries very hard and encapsulates the rust. In fact, it needs rust to work. POR-15 and similar products are available at automotive paint supply stores. It is hygroscopic and reacts with the air. If you don't put a product like Saran Wrap between the lid and can, you will never get the can open a second time.

Wear plastic gloves and an old shirt since you apply this overhead. If it gets on your skin, it will take weeks to remove. This is tough stuff.

Paint the tunnel area before installing the floor pan.

The POR-15 products have been recommended by many 356 restorers. We don't use a lot of POR-15 products since we have all the areas to be repaired on a 356 media blasted, so there is no rust.

Now for the floor installation. First mask off the floor pan and paint the area that will be the tunnel floor. Measure and mark off the area so you won't be painting where you will be welding the floor to the tunnel ledge. You cannot weld a painted area. You can't use POR-15 for this application, since the replacement floor pan has no rust. Instead, use a two-part epoxy primer and apply it with a bottle sprayer. The two-part epoxy paint is available from various auto paint manufacturers. They are all similar.

We use PPG's DP-90 product, which is a satin black. The bottle sprayer is made by Preval and is available at most hardware stores. They are inexpensive, about $6, and replacement power units are about $5. We use a lot of these when painting small parts. They are quicker to use than preparing and cleaning the spray gun. In fact, when our spray gun was in for repair, we painted the whole underside of a 356 with the bottle sprayer and six power units.

POR-15 is the pint sized can. The other products are discussed in the text.

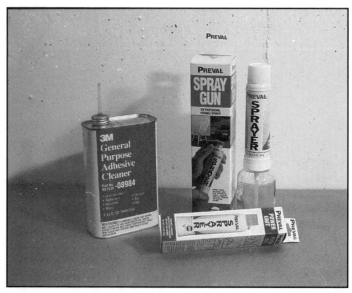

The Preval sprayer and our favorite cleaning product.

When mixing and applying the two-part epoxy paint, you must wear a respirator. Buy a good respirator when you get the paint at the auto paint store. They are not expensive. Mix the paint according to directions. With DP-90, you have a choice of catalysts; one allows immediate use of the paint but only has a 24-hour pot life. With the other catalyst, you have to wait an hour before applying, but you have a 72-hour pot life. Pot life is the time before the paint sets up and is unusable. It can be extended some by refrigeration. Only mix up enough paint for the jobs at hand. You will have to dilute the paint with a reducer (recommended by your paint store), about 20 percent to get it to spray with the Preval unit. After using, clean the Preval unit by running lacquer thinner through it and removing the spray cap. Directions are on the box.

The floor pan is now ready for installation. It will have to be trimmed to fit. With a piece of plywood under the floor pan and on your jack, position the floor pan in the opening. Line it up with the pattern on the front floor pan and center it. Mark the edges and back of the floor pan with a scratch awl or marking pen by scribing around the ledges and back edges. You can mark the tunnel ledges for centering purposes. If you left the transverse tube in place, scribe at the back of the tube. If you cut it out, you do not need to make a scribe. At the back of the floor pan, mark where the rear of the tunnel meets the floor pan.

Time to cheat here. When you cut out the floor pan from under the tunnel, you left some of the floor pan on top of the rear ledge because you could not grind it off, as it was under the tunnel. Cut the floor pan so you can bend down the floor pan area under the tunnel and slide this part of the floor pan underneath. Mark this junction to cut in an inch and a quarter. If you left in the rear seat mounts, you will have to mark for similar cuts. The seat mounts are still attached to the sides and can be bent up. Now remove the pan. If your side ledges are three-quarters of an inch all around, all you have to do is make another line about five-eighths of an inch outside your line.

If your ledges are irregular in width, you can cut out strips of paper/cardboard that match the shape and transfer them to the floor pan and cut back in one-eighth of an inch. At the back of the floor pan, extend the line out an inch. You need to do nothing in front.

Now, you can trim on your new outside lines. Use an electric shear (easier, quicker) or do it by hand with tin snips. Make short one and one-quarter inch cuts to go under the tunnel and under the seat mounts. As mentioned earlier, if the floor pan has galvanizing material on it, it will have to be removed from the edges with a grinder. You will also have to decide on the welding technique to use. You can simulate spot welds or seam weld the floor pan. If you are going to simulate spot welds, you need to punch the holes on the side and back edges of your replacement floor pan and also on the tunnel ledge now. They should be done about every inch, but vary this to get a random look. You

can drill the holes; use a manual punch or an air punch. The diameter of the holes should be about three-sixteenths of an inch. If you are going to seam weld, you need do no more.

Now, as you noticed during removal, the floor pan has to go up above the side ledges and up over the rear ledge except for that short section that goes under the tunnel. To accomplish this, put a bend in the floor pan by standing in the middle on your painted tunnel part and pull up on the sides.

Place the slightly bent floor pan on your plywood and jack and place in the opening. Lift up enough to get the sides onto the ledges, then push back to start the back edge over the ledge. Now, bend down the section that will go under the rear tunnel ledge. Use the jack to push up the floor pan. The clearance and fit problems will be evident. Seldom will you get the rear floor pan to fit in the first try. Remove, trim and reinstall until the floor pan is in place and you have a nice tight seam on the edges.

Not only do you want fairly tight side seams, you want the floor pan flush with the side ledges. If it is not, support it underneath with a 2 x 4 on your floor jack and use a hammer and block of wood to force it down. You can use sheet metal screws to secure the floor pan to the ledge. Remove the screws and weld the holes later. The floor pan has to be flush with the ledges for a plug weld and you have to see clean shiny metal under your punched holes.

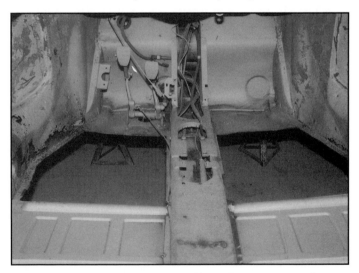

Rear floor pan tacked in place and front floor pan started. Note that the pedal cluster on this early 356 is welded to the floor. Since there was no rust damage in this area (unusual), we are going to patch the floor pan after damage to the inner longitudinals is repaired.

You can now proceed with your plug welds. Alternate holes a foot apart and ensure each is flush. If seam welding, you can tack weld the floor to the edges about every six to eight inches, alternating around and ensuring the floor pan is flush to the ledges. Then finish your side and back welds. If the front floor pan will not be replaced, you can butt weld to the back of the transverse tube. If the

Completed floor pans with plug welds yet to be ground. Note we didn't take our own advice and the instrument bulb string was left dangling.

front floor pan will be replaced, only weld up to within six inches of the tube area. Either grind your welds now or save it for a grinding party when you've finished the front floor pan. Hey, step back and admire your work. The new rear floor pan looks great, doesn't it?

Front Floor Pan

This will be very similar to the rear floor pan; the front bulkhead area may have damage. Mud gets trapped on top of the diagonal piece (1956-65) that is welded to the bottom of the front bulkhead and causes rust damage. If this happened, cut and remove the diagonal piece from under the 356. You will repair it later. Another area of rust damage occurs when mud gets trapped at the back of the front struts (mid 1956-65), the area below the openings for the tie rods. Once the rust starts in this area, it not only takes out the struts, it gets into the front bulkhead. There is also a tar paper-like insulation on the interior of the front bulkhead. This will have to be cut back and removed. Any tar residue plus melting tar can ruin your weld.

A replacement panel for the front bulkhead is available. The condition of the bulkhead will indicate replacement or repair. A repair to the bulkhead under the tunnel area will have to be done from under the car in most cases, but first the front floor pan must be cut out. Once again, decide if the seat rail mounts are salvageable. Cut out the front floor pan as you did the rear, staying out an inch from the edges. At the front bulkhead will be a lip that the floor pan sits on. Cut one inch back from this lip. Use the side cutter to remove the floor pan under the tunnel. There may be a reinforcing bracket in the tunnel behind the shifter that is welded to the floor pan. Mark its location and cut around it. With the front floor pan out, see if the bracket that holds the pedal cluster is salvageable. Save all the sheet metal you cut off during your restoration. It makes a neat picture

Save the rusty sheet metal for a reminder photo.

laid along side your finished 356. There is usually a piece that will make an interesting wall hanging for the garage.

Repair the front side ledges as you did the rear. For the front bulkhead, you may have to make a curved piece. Make your pattern; cut out your repair piece and hand bend it to approximate the curve. When you tack it in, start at one end and tack both sides. Ensure the patch is flush for the next inch and tack. Do this again. You are fitting the curve to the original good metal on either side.

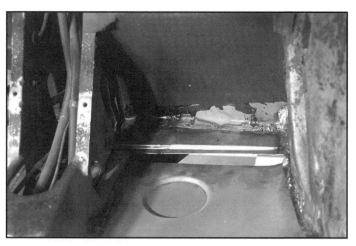

Part of the front floor bulkhead has been fabricated; fortunately not much of the curved area had to be replicated. Note that it has been flanged to receive the floor pan which sits on top.

Installation of the front floor pan is the same as the rear, but don't forget to paint the tunnel and the area under the tunnel prior to installation. You also need to line up the rear groove on the front floor pan with the groove on the rear floor pan to create the transverse tube. Welding this tube will be fun as you will be welding new metal to new metal. You should be able to lay down a perfect weld.

You can now install the pedal cluster bracket. Attach the pedal cluster to the master cylinder. Ensure it is centered by lining up the clutch cable pivot with the clutch cable and mark for the three holes in the floor. Drill the holes, insert the bracket under the floor and attach to the pedal cluster. Tack weld the bracket to the bottom of the floor.

Trial fit of the front floor pan. It will be marked and trimmed to fit.

Front floor pan installed. Welds will be ground. The floor painted with two-part epoxy paint and all seams caulked. Torn tarpaper will be replaced.

The factory used about one-half inch tack welds a few inches apart. Remove the pedal cluster. If you removed the seat mounts, there are replacement pieces available. To properly position them, you will need to put the rails on the tunnel and line them up with the outboard seat rails. There should be a straight line across all four rails. On pre-1962 cars, the front of the rail is determined by the little notch that the seat slides into. Use the seat bottom to position the width between rails. With everything lined up, tack the seat mounts into place. Remove the seat bottom and rails and finish the welds. Now install the toe board mounts. Some toe board mounts have holes that go over two of the studs on the pedal cluster bracket; others have to be notched to fit up against the pedal cluster bracket. You can use your floor boards and pedal cluster bracket to position them. Tack weld in place. Many times you will see the driver side toe board mount with the captive nuts for the accelerator pedal also installed on the passenger side. After the front floor pan is in, hang your doors to ensure they are still centered. Then maybe invite some friends over for a floor pan party!

Lock Post

There may be rust damage at the bottom of the lock post where it meets the threshold. There also may be damage in the leaded area where the lock post meets the outer quarter panel skin. Look behind the lock post to determine rust damage. If present, you will have to remove all the lead using the techniques described earlier. (Don't forget the sermon!) If there is more than minor damage in this area, it means lock post replacement. This is one of the trickiest repairs on a 356. Hopefully you will only need a repair at the bottom. If your 356 has the round indentation at the bottom and you have to repair this area, you can make the indentation in your repair piece by pounding on a socket of the proper size or squeezing between two different size sockets in a vise.

This lock post will have to be replaced.

To replace the lock post, you should have the replacement piece in hand prior to removing the original damaged panel. You will notice that the replacement lock post extends below the threshold. It also doesn't have the crisp edges that the factory created with lead. After studying the replacement lock post, you should be able to determine where to make your cuts. One cut will be inside on the inner fender so that the channels for the door seal line up.

Before removing the lock post, make some reference marks on the outer skin to indicate the top and bottom of the recess area on the lock post. This is the area where the striker plate is attached. With the old lock post removed, use the door as a jig. Make sure your hinge pins are almost all the way in. If not, sometimes when you finally seat them, the door will move in position. It may not be to the position you planned. The reason the lock post is tricky is that it leans back and angles outward to allow the door to shut. Before installing the lock post, use the old lock post as a pattern to drill holes for the striker plate. Also clean all your edges to clean shiny metal on both the lock post and lock post opening.

Place the new lock post in the opening and do any necessary trimming. When it fits tight in the opening and lines up with your reference marks, close the door and check for an even gap at the back of the door. When you get an even gap, tack weld the lock post in place with only four to six tacks.

Now install the latch assembly in the door and the striker plate on the lock post. With these in place, slowly close the door and see if the top of the door latch is just going to clear the top of the striker plate. Adjust the striker plate until it does. Gently shut the door; remember the lock post is only secured with tack welds. Adjust the striker plate until the door latches and the door is flush to the lock post. You may have to file or use a rotary tool on the holes on the lock post to make adjustments. To open the door, use your finger in the door handle hole to trip the latch. Once the door latches and is flush at the lock post, weld the lock post in place. Leave the door latch mechanism and striker plate in place to secure the door.

Threshold/Rocker

If the threshold is not totally rusted out, you should be able to patch it. Most of the damage occurs to the inside where the U channel in the door seal rusts. These areas can be patched, although you will not be able to get your welding tip back into the rear threshold channel. Use JB Weld or other good two-part putty to seal the area. *We use two-part epoxy plumber's putty. It dries hard and looks like lead.*

This threshold can be patched.

If you decide to replace the threshold, also evaluate the rocker panel. You can buy a combination threshold/rocker panel for a one-step replacement. In either case, you are going to use the door bottom as a jig to get the edge of the threshold properly gapped and flush. The rocker, as either part of the threshold/rocker assembly or as a stand alone piece, is not a drop in installation. It may appear a little long or short on either end. This means you will have to center it and re-contour where the rocker meets the front and rear wheel opening.

The area where the rocker joins the fenders originally had an overlap area and the rocker was spot welded to the fender and then leaded over. As the undercoat disap-

peared behind this area, moisture could get into the seam and cause rust damage. *We prefer to trim the overlap and butt weld the rockers to the fender.* If you use the original design, you will have to ensure this area is adequately protected when you paint, caulk and undercoat the underbody.

During this repair, the rocker panel has been butt welded to the lower part of the front fender.

Another area of the threshold or threshold/rocker assembly that can be used as a jig is the hole in the threshold to access the lower door hinge pin. You can use a drift through the access hole to the lower hinge to assist in positioning the threshold. Once the threshold is installed, move to the front door pocket area for possible additional repairs. There is a triangular piece at the front of the threshold that is spot welded on top of the threshold, under the inner panel and ledged to the front closing panel. If the front closing panel is rust damaged, the piece may also be damaged. You can fabricate this piece.

A repair to the inner front threshold area is facilitated by having the fender repair done later. An example of working from the center outward.

Front Closing Panels

The closing panel is where the rust starts. A rock is thrown up by the front wheel. It wears off the undercoat. Rust

Looks like we can patch the inner section and replace the outer lower section. We will also have to patch behind the outer section. We will scribe the overlap curve before removing the damaged outer section.

starts. Then there is a small hole. Moisture gets in the longitudinal. Then a bigger hole and more moisture in the longitudinal. And away it goes! The front closing panel is made up of two pieces overlapping at a nice vertical curve and spot-welded. There are also ribs and circle impressions on the outer part of the closing panel. If rust damage has not gotten into the overlap curve or impressions, the closing panel can be easily patched. However, if the rust damage is also in the seam between the closing panel and fender, it is best to replace the closing panel. You can get closing panels to match most of the impressions. You can also get just the lower half.

Installation of the complete panel is very complex, particularly in the upper areas, which are more easily done with the front fender off. If you have extensive damage to the closing panel, you might get a complete panel and cut it to only use areas to replace damaged metal. To work on the section of the closing panel that attaches to the fender, you will use the door again as a jig to keep the fender flush with the door. The curve on your replacement closing panel may force the fender out, not allowing the fender to fit flush. You may have to make cuts on the curved area of the closing panel in order to bend it in and get it flush to the door. Do careful work with the closing panel. You want the repair pieces to fit flush to the remaining good metal. After grinding you want the weld on the closing panel to disappear as this area is visible when the wheels are turned.

Longitudinal

Rust damage here is usually at the front closing panel, rear closing panel and under the jack spur. Once again, you need to determine if it can be patched or needs replacement. If you decide to patch, you may want to buy a longitudinal to get your repair pieces due to the outer curve, which is tough to form by hand. If you are going to

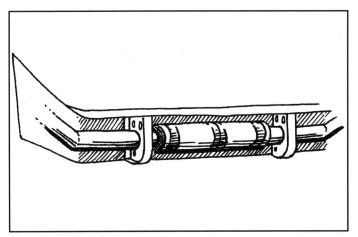

Support pieces in longitudinal.

replace it, it may be necessary to also replace the interior support pieces and heating tubes.

Now, to be totally correct, the longitudinal should have been replaced prior to the threshold repair/replacement. If you look at the sill where the aluminum threshold rail was that covered the carpet, you will see three layers of metal. The top is the inner longitudinal, the middle is the outer longitudinal, and the bottom, the threshold.

By replacing the longitudinal now, this sequence of repair is compatible with the idea of patching, rather than replacing when possible and not disturbing good factory seams. Plus, it is easier for the first time restorer. If this is of concern, back up to the beginning of the threshold repair, drill out the 70 or so spot welds through three layers of metal and replace the longitudinal at that time. Yes, this would be a time-consuming repair which is why we suggest the following technique.

To remove the longitudinal, take a look where the longitudinal sits under your new floor pan. Cut back from this edge about an inch and a quarter. With your cutting tool, cut up as high as you can on the vertical piece that goes up to the sill. With some minor cutting on the ends, the longitudinal, or what is left of it, will fall to the floor. You can

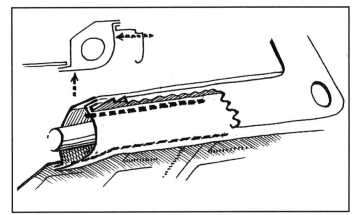

Cutting out the longitudinal:
1) Cut longitudinal back from where new floor pan is welded to the inner ledge.
2) Cut the vertical piece of the longitudinal under the threshold.

now inspect the cavity. The support pieces that hold the heating tubes are available. If replacing them, you will have to cut them to fit around the heat tubes, if not replacing the tubes. Before removing the support pieces, measure their depth and make sure it is the same on the replacement. This piece butts up to, but is not welded to, the longitudinal.

After the repairs are made in the cavity, it should be painted. If rust is present, use a rust neutralizer or POR-15. If this area got blasted because most of the longitudinal was missing, use two-part epoxy paint. On your replacement longitudinal, cut off the top ledge that would become the sill. Mask off the edges where you will weld and paint the inside with two-part epoxy paint. Also paint the back of the front closing panel. You need to grind flush the remains of the longitudinal under the inner longitudinal ledge. Now you can install the longitudinal. Push the vertical part up into the seam where you made your upper cut. Support the longitudinal with a 2 x 4 on your floor jack. Trim any areas of interference. Make sure you are tight to the front closing panel. If the longitudinal doesn't look flush and correct, you may have to trim the vertical area and reinsert into the seam. By gently lifting with the jack, you can also get the horizontal edge to meet the floor pan. Be careful. You don't want to dent the longitudinal. When all looks correct, tack weld into place, then finish with seam welds. You are going to cheat a little and tack weld the vertical area to the bottom of the threshold. Later, after bottom paint, you will caulk between tack welds and make the repair invisible.

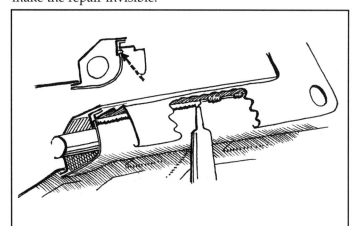

Caulking between longitudinal tacks:
1) Tack welds securing vertical section of longitudinal to bottom of threshold. Caulk between tack welds to close off this area.

Jack Spur

Jack spurs usually need to be replaced even if the longitudinal is in good shape. They get crushed by road hazards and use. There are three styles, detailed in *Authenticity*. Placement on the later 356s is 210 mm from the end of the longitudinal to the edge of the jack spur. On real early 356s, it is 290 mm. You want the jack spur to clear the rocker by about one-half inch or less. Paint inside the jack

spur with two-part epoxy paint. Mask off the edges. Use a small jack to hold in place and plug weld or seam weld to the longitudinal. Reproduction jack spurs may take some work to fit to the curve of the longitudinal. This is the last time you will touch the jack spur as you should never use it to jack the 356. Buy an inexpensive scissor or hydraulic jack to use if needed while traveling. It is too easy to damage your car by using the original jack to risk it.

Rear Closing Panel

Usually if there is damage to the rear closing panel, it is just as easy to replace as repair. Make sure you get the panel that is correct for your 356. Cut out the old closing panel, paint the back of the replacement and trim and bend into place as required. At the inner rear fender, there are factory overlap seams that may be rusted out. Rather than trying to replace the overlap, you should grind down the damage and repair. This completes the major stuff on the sides of the 356.

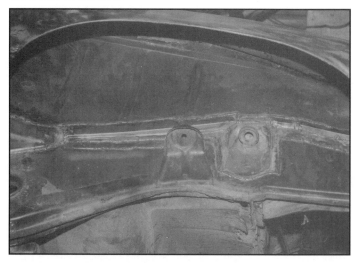

Repairs to factory overlap seams in rear inner fender

We missed this damage to the rear inner fender when we did the evaluation. The cardboard backing of the upholstery side panel had been undercoated to look like metal. What probably happened is that the 356 was driven in the rain with the quarter window open. Moisture got behind the side panel and was trapped by the glue securing the side panel to the inner fender.

Battery Box

Damage can occur just to the area under the battery due to acid leakage, just to the floor due to misuse of a jack or to the floor and sides due to neglect. If damage is just under the battery, you can make a patch. You will still have to buy a new panel, but just use what you need for a patch. The patch will be similar to the floor pan patch. Try to save factory welds and seams if not damaged and make your cut on the high point of an impression, again, like a floor patch. When replacing the whole battery floor, make your cuts in from the ledge and then grind down the remaining floor on the ledge. It is best to use plug welds on the battery box floor as this is a visible area.

Battery floor installed.

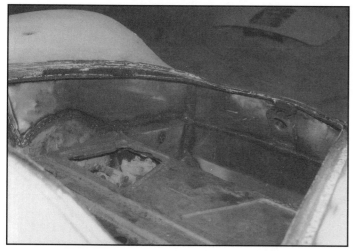

Major repairs to the battery box area and front compartment.

If there is damage on the sides of the battery box, it may include the brackets for the attachment of the front bumper. These brackets and panels are readily available. Under the battery box is the tow hook except on cars earlier than the 1958 model year. Often this can be saved and reused. Rivets are available. Reproduction tow hooks are not identical to the original. To install/reinstall the tow hook, drill the appropriate holes in the battery box floor, using the tow hook bracket for alignment. Secure the tow hook with bolts. Remove a bolt, insert a rivet and trim the

rivet so there is only about one-quarter inch to peen down. Make a tool out of a long steel rod by drilling an indent in one end to sit over the rivet head. Have a friend hold the rod on the rivet while you peen the rivet with a ball peen hammer from underneath. The rivet is soft metal and easy to work; make sure to get it tight.

On early 356s, there are vertical triangular pieces on both sides of the center recess to secure the battery and provide for the spring and clips that secure the battery cover. If these are missing or need repair, an illustration and measurements are on page 311 of the *Restoration Guide*.

Diagonal

The next repair up front could be the diagonal. For later 356s, this is usually a drop-in piece, i.e. needs no trimming. The old diagonal would have been removed at the rear if you had replaced the front floor pan and worked on the bulkhead. The diagonal is welded in front at the sway bar mounting brackets. You will have to reposition your jack stands to remove the sway bar. Be careful removing the sway bar mounting bolts. While they go through a substantial piece of metal, the end threads are exposed and in an area that collects dirt. Clean out the area above the bolts before removing them. With the sway bar and brackets off, you can see the factory weld. Cut this with a side cutter and trim as necessary, using your replacement diagonal as a pattern. Welding in the diagonal is straightforward except at the back. There is a small depression that serves as a drain, so leave room in the middle of your rear weld for the drain. For early 356s, the diagonal is two pieces that attach at the rear to the boxed in area of the front tunnel. This area is often damaged by jacking. If the flat center section needs to be replaced, use 18-gauge metal.

Struts

The front struts, along with the diagonal, are very important to the integrity of the front chassis. The front strut is the horizontal piece below the opening for the tie rods on each side. It is an L shaped or boxed piece, depending on the 356 model. It, along with the diagonal, ties the front end to the chassis. Unless damage is minimal, they should be replaced. On early 356s (prior to mid-1956), the strut is open and is a mud trap. On later 356s (from mid-1956), it is boxed. Usually, you have to repair the metal to which the strut is attached. When affixing the strut, plug welds are recommended.

Fender Braces/Headlight Bucket

Rear fender brace replacement is straightforward; just mark the position before removal for reattachment. Front fender braces are more of a challenge. If just the outer end is damaged, you can weld in sections from a replacement brace. If the fender brace has to be replaced, you will have to remove the wires that go to the headlight. After remov-

Headlight wires go from the headlight bucket through the fender brace and into the front compartment.

ing the headlight bulb socket, pull the wires from inside the front compartment. If jammed by dirt, use a stiff wire and air to blow out the dirt. Don't add liquid as all you can make is mud. Once you get some slack, you can pull the wires back and forth to work out the dirt.

Removal of the fender brace is made easier if the bottom of the headlight bucket has been rusted out. If not, cut the tube below the headlight bucket, trim your replacement to match and make your weld. Use a piece of aluminum tubing inserted into the fender brace tube to prevent cat's whiskers inside. If just the bottom of the headlight bucket is shot, you can make this repair after installing the new front fender brace. You want the top of the fender brace tube to extend into the headlight bucket about an inch.

If replacing the headlight bucket, drill out the spot welds that secure it to the fender. Prior to installing the new headlight bucket, make some cuts diagonally around the bottom hole and bend down to make installation over the fender brace tube easier. Use the rubber seal and headlight chrome rim as a jig when positioning the headlight bucket in the opening. Also, drill or punch your holes for plug welds prior to installation. Install and weld the headlight bucket, then the fender brace, and bend up and weld the cuts you made in the bottom.

We agreed to help with the installation of a headlight bucket for a friend doing his own restoration. At the time, 356 headlight buckets were not available and you were offered 911 headlight buckets, but they don't look right on a 356. So I suggested he go to a VW junkyard and get a headlight bucket. He came back with a complete front fender. It cost him $20. We removed the headlight bucket from the fender and installed it in his 356. Later he took the fender sans headlight bucket to another VW junkyard and got $25 for it!

You will have to decide if you will be restoring or replacing your headlight assembly. The issue is the replacement

headlight assembly has advantages but doesn't fit. The advantage is you get a complete (except for bulb) new assembly: new glass, new chrome trim ring and new painted housing. If you are going with replacement assemblies, you will have to obtain them and modify your headlight bucket to make them fit. Modification of the headlight bucket involves bending the edge of the bucket inward and grinding down the edge so the replacement assembly fits flush to the body allowing for the rubber seal.

If you will be restoring your headlight assembly, you can dry fit it again, making sure it will fit flush. Restoring the headlight assembly may involve re-chroming the trim ring, replacing the glass and repainting the housing.

With both the original and replacement headlights, be careful removing or installing the retaining clips. Wear eye protection!

Rear Strut

This is the area below the rear torsion tube. This is the lowest part of the 356 and if the longitudinal was rusted out, this area probably needs repair. This is another area where 18-gauge metal should be used. If damage is up

Damage to the right rear lower strut. Note that this area is hollow and is the lowest part of the chassis. Rust has destroyed one of the captive nuts, for the torsion bar cover bolt (cover is at jack stand). The repair approach would be to make patterns of the metal to be replaced. Then, remove the damaged metal. Treat rusty metal in the hollow area with a rust neutralizer. Fabricate a new captive nut using the remaining nuts as a model. Position the new captive nut using the cover as a guide. Then, fabricate the inner sides, outer side and bottom pieces using patterns, and tack into place. Eighteen gauge metal would be appropriate in this area.

into the area of the bolts securing the torsion tube cover, the trailing arm will have to be removed. Scribe a line on the chassis to assist in reinstallation. This area of repair can be very difficult, depending on the amount of damage. The higher up the damage the more fabrication is required to correctly position the trailing arm bolt locations. What helps is to make patterns from an undamaged 356.

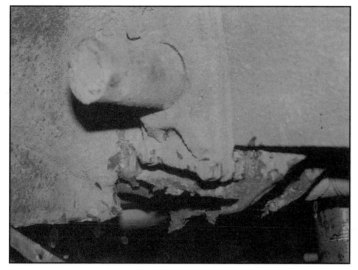

Another rear strut damaged by rust. One problem here will be removing the lower cover bolts without doing further damage to the area. Since the area is hollow, the bolt ends will be exposed allowing cleaning, penetrating solvent, and heat.

That covers most of the common repairs under the 356. Now it is time for some of the exterior repairs.

Hood

We have probably evaluated over 100 hoods. We have only found a few virgins. Some of the ugliest repairs we've seen have been in the hood hinge brace area. Before starting on the hood, check the hinge pockets. When you removed the hood hinge, you may have seen damage at the bottom of the pocket. This needs to be repaired now. This is usually damage to the factory weld and it can be cleaned and re-welded.

The hood has probably been kinked. If the kink is minor i.e. no rips in the hood channel, you may be able to force it

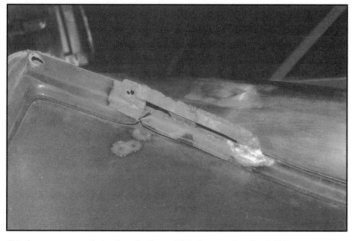

We have seen a lot of ugly hood kink repairs, but this was our favorite. Usually there are pieces of rebar brazed in this area. This winner has an ugly piece of metal brazed over the hood kink damage. Note the hole (drain?) in the rear corner. Repair in this area was done as described in the hood repair section. The ugly repair was removed by carefully bending the metal with a vice grip until the soft brazing separated from the hood channel.

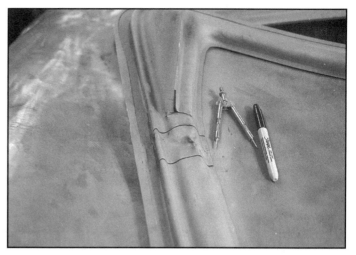

Prior to cutting through the kink area, we use dividers to ensure a parallel cut.

into position. Use a broom stick crosswise in the fender channel for the hood seal below the high spot on the hood. With two people, press down on the high spots simultaneously and see if you can force it into position. Metal has a memory and it may return to its proper position. If the hood is too high at the cowl area, place the hood on the floor with wax paper under the hinge bracket so it will slide and in your stocking feet, step down on the high spot. Place the hood back on the car and see if it is flush with the cowl. Previous repairs to the kinked area may consist of brazing and rebar.

To repair this, cut through the kink area. Place the hood in the opening and tack it flush in four areas. Next, use four pieces of square tubing with legs on each end. Tack weld these on both sides of the centerline of the hood. This temporary support will hold the hood in position for making

The support piece that holds the hood in position.

the repair. Remove the four tack welds securing the hood to the fenders and place the hood upside down with the tubing still in place. Remove the damaged area of the hood channel by cutting a piece with parallel edges. Cut a repair piece that is the width of the removed channel piece and a little bit longer so it will fit the curves in the channel. Fit

Tacking the repair piece while following the hood channel curve.

the repair piece to the first curve of the inside part of the channel and tack it to the inside sides of the channel. Push down the repair piece to meet the curve and tack again. Do this until you meet the valley between the inner curve and smaller outer curve. Then bend your repair piece to match the smaller curve and trim your end to meet the outer edge of the channel. Tack the repair piece to the small curve and outer edge, then finish your welds. Grind welds with a die grinder. Remove your support tubes on the outer hood and you're done.

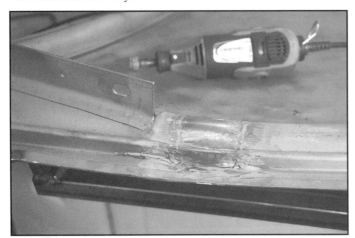

Hood kink repaired.

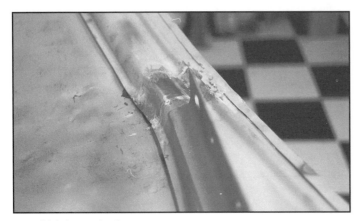

Hood kink repaired.

There may be rust damage to the inner nose of the hood. This can be caused by incorrect installation of the hood seal. If the point of the *V* of the seal is placed outward, the seal will hold water when the 356 is wet. When the hood is closed, it sits in a pool of water. If the rust holes are small, they can be filled with JB Weld or similar two-part putty. If there is more extensive damage, you will need a replacement hood or professional repair.

We had restored a 356 for a customer including kinked hood repair. He really enjoyed driving his 356. Years later, as a Christmas gift, his wife gave him a gift certificate to have his 356 professionally detailed. While he indicated to the shop management the opening and closing of the hood, you guessed it, the teenager in the shop kinked the hood. So we got to repair and repaint the hood a second time. The detail shop did pay for the repair.

Doors

You have been using the doors for jigs, even though they may be damaged. Other than dents, there may be previous repairs, including brazing. Rust damage usually occurs to the door bottom and bottom door skin. Start with the door bottom first. If most of the metal is still there, you can patch it using pieces from a replacement part or sheet stock. If you have to replace the whole bottom, the panel that is available is almost a drop in. You have to drill out quite a few spot welds and pull metal back until you can fit the piece. Bend the metal back and plug weld through the spot weld holes.

Bottom door panel replacement. This repair panel is an almost exact replacement. Once spot welds are drilled out and the rusted panel removed, it is almost a drop-in repair.

The bottom door skin is another story. We have had mixed success trying to butt weld in this piece. Now we use a ledging or flanging tool to create a lip on the door skin to receive the repair piece.

It is important to get the fold-over crease properly positioned on the door bottom before making and cutting the

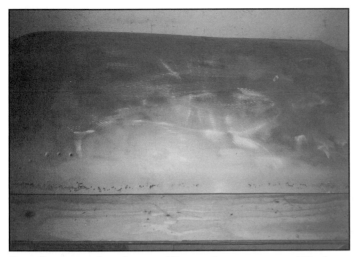

Rust damage at door bottom. We can also see some pull holes from a previous repair.

Using a straight edge and plasma cutter to remove rust damaged door skin.

A flanging tool is used to create a lip for the replacement door bottom skin. Note also that the inner panel had to be repaired and this door will need rust treatment on the interior.

repair piece to fit on the door skin lip. Hang the door to ensure a good bottom gap. Welding this piece will take time as you have to let each short weld cool before doing

Tack welding the door bottom skin. Note fan to cool area and avoid warpage when doing finish welds.

another in a different area. Don't use a wet rag to speed up cooling. This will warp the door skin and cause brittle welds. Use a fan and have other projects to do as you wait. After you have repaired the door, install your old door seal and ensure the door will close flush.

Even though the door gaps haven't been worked on yet, it is necessary to know the door will shut flush. If it doesn't, determine where it is too tight and move metal around the door opening until it does. Most interference will be at the front. You can close the door with a piece of paper between it and the seal. The paper should pull out with a slight drag.

Fenders

Rust damage to the front fender usually occurs at the top rear, in front of the door and around the headlight bucket. The top rear damage is due to mud buildup on the upper ledge of the front closing panel and the amount of bare

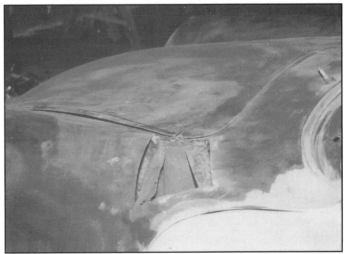

The top of the front closing panel acts as a mud trap. Here part of the fender has been cut away to make a repair. After repair and repaint underneath, a half tube of caulk can be applied to turn the ledge at the top of the front closing panel into a sloped surface that won't trap mud.

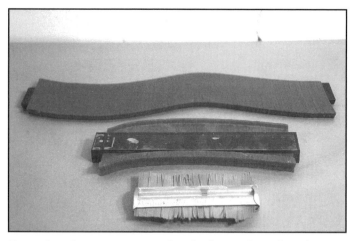

Examples of contour gauges; the plastic type is preferred.

metal overlap used by the factory. Repairs in this area are tricky due to the compound curves. A tool to use in getting these curves correct is a woodworker's contour gauge. This is a plastic or metal tool with numerous teeth. By pressing it on a curve on a correct side and turning it around, you can replicate the curve on the other side. There is a repair piece available that can be used for both the front of the door and top of the fender.

This was something else! The rear fender on this coupe was replaced with a fender from an open 356. Of course the curve was wrong, so it was fixed with bondo. Up to 1" thick! It took an air chisel to get it off. The area was repaired by cutting a seam at the low point. Then with marks about an inch apart on the good side replicated on the damaged side, the metal was pulled up to meet a contour taken from the good side. A contour gauge was used. The area was tack welded and the next area pulled up and tacked using the contour gauge numerous times. We were fortunate that the excess metal from the open 356 fender was not cut off. It was left under the car.

There is also available a circular repair piece for the fender around the headlight bucket. This is also a tricky repair as you have to trim and tack in the repair piece, then use your bucket and front fender brace as a jig. You can use a long straight edge to ensure the headlight bucket is positioned correctly. Hold it across the buckets with hood open or off to determine equal position. Rear fender damage is usually behind the doors and would have been repaired as part of the lockpost repair.

General Exterior Damage

Other damage to the outer skin can be due to collision damage or storage dents. Small dents can be pulled into place using the stud welder or by hammering from behind and checking curves with the contour gauge. Deep dents with a crease may require cutting through the crease, pulling metal into place and welding the cut. Use of a body hammer and dolly will assist in getting the metal flush. Use sandpaper to determine high spots, they will be shiny. Work down with a body hammer.

The techniques for using metal working tools are described in numerous books on auto body repair. If you wish to attempt this type of work on your own, you should obtain one of these books and practice the techniques on discarded damaged panels available from most body shops at no cost.

Often metal will be stretched in a dented area after it's been pulled or pushed out and will have to be shrunk. Have a bucket of water with a shop towel ready and always wear gloves. Use your propane torch to get a spot the size of a nickel cherry red, then quench with water. Don't overdo it as too much heat will cause the metal to change character and become brittle. Let the area air cool.

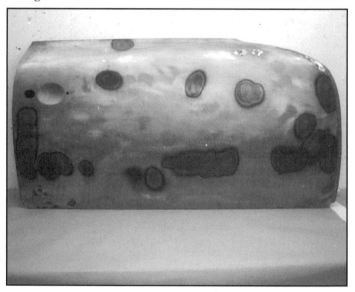

Heat treatment to shrink metal that has been stretched by dents.

A common area of repair on later 356s is between the horn grilles. There is a flat bracket behind this area to secure the upper horn grille and optional fog lights. Since the bracket is flat and the outer skin curved, it is a natural mud trap. After repair, ensure this area is caulked after painting under the car.

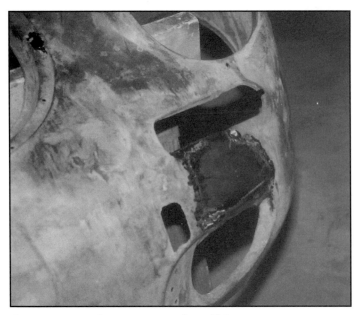

A common rust damage area on later 356s.

Bumpers

You evaluated your bumpers when they were disassembled. Other than dents and rust damage, the most common problem is the spinners previously mentioned. This is when damage occurs to the captive nut and it just spins. The nut is welded to a small square piece of metal and held in place by side keepers. To repair this area, you will have to cut out the metal over the nut. Save this piece as a pattern for a replacement piece with the proper size and positioned access hole. Once opened, you can see the required repairs to the side keepers. Make the repair and test with captive nut you've made before fabricating and welding in a new top piece. A captive nut is easy to make by drilling a hole in a square of sheet metal and welding a nut over the hole. Sometimes the bumper bolt shears, but the captive nut is still good. Rather than attempt to drill out and tap for the bolt, the above repair is quicker.

After repairs, dry fit the bumpers. Attach your bumper brackets and install on the car. If you have over-rider tubes or guards on your bumpers, now would be the time to fit them also. If they had been damaged and repaired or just re-chromed, you want to ensure proper fit before paint. You want the bumper brackets to exit in the center of the bracket opening and the bumper to have the same end distance from the body. For the 1960-65 356, where the rear bumper ends are secured to the rear fender brace, you want the ends to touch equally.

The installation sequence for the end pieces on the 1960-65 bumper is as follows (many have been reinstalled wrong): The rubber pieces are installed flat side to the body; one on the outside, one inside. The metal sleeve goes through the rubber pieces and protrudes to the inside where it is covered by the metal washer cap. The bolt with washer runs through the bracket on the rear fender brace and through the sleeve to the captive nut on the bumper.

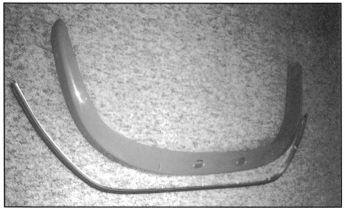

Reproduction bumper trim may not match the curve of the bumper.

Adjustments can be made with the slots for the bolts on the brackets.

If you are using reproduction bumper deco, you will notice they may not fit the curve of the bumper. It may be bent about a foot from the ends. The ends also may be bent out. Reproduction bumper decos come with non-metric carriage bolts, which could rotate in the aluminum channel. We either replace these bolts or are careful not to secure them multiple times. To remove the incorrect bend in the deco, pull out the rubber insert in the area. With a narrow piece of one inch bar about a foot long, secure it to the deco with a clamp.

We use a locking C clamp. By tightening the clamp, you can work the bend out. To bend in the ends, we protect them and bend in a vise. Dry fit to the bumper to ensure fit. Reinstall carriage bolts and rubber insert, use a craft stick to push the rubber insert into place. Get the ends seated first.

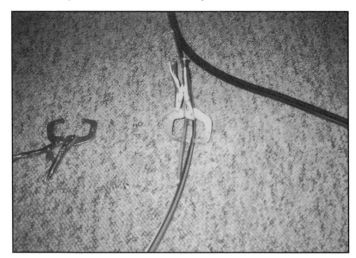

Getting the correct bend in bumper deco.

Rear Deck Lid

The rear deck lid seldom needs repair. As mentioned earlier, it pops up in a rear collision. There is rarely rust damage to the rear lid. But there may be dents and this can be fixed using previously discussed techniques.

A customer who lived in the Colorado mountains stored his 356 outside under a pipe frame and canvas cover. He secured the pipe frame to the 356 with a rope around the rear deck lid. Well, during heavy winds, the rope bent the rear lid and the pipes dented the 356. This was one of the few times we had to replace a rear lid. Most of the problem was getting the replacement rear lid to fit in the opening as originals were fit by hand at the factory.

Roof

Usually, the only rust damage to the roof is at the factory welds above the fender behind the quarter window. This is an overlap seam similar to the rocker to fender overlap. If the 356 was driven in the rain with the quarter window open, water would get under the headliner and into this seam. The rust repair in this area is the same as other repairs, and a butt weld is preferred.

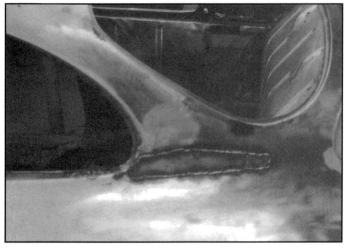

This is the area between the roof and the rear fender where the factory had a flange and overlap weld. A caulk was applied that would dry and shrink. If the 356 was driven in the wet with the quarter window open, moisture could get behind the head liner and cause rust damage to the seam.

While open 356s don't have a roof, they can also have problems caused by rain. Putting down a wet top causes water to run down the top creases and into the top hinge area. The curved side panels behind the door opening have foam rubber under the vinyl and once this sponge gets wet, the panel can be damaged. Rust repairs in these areas are tricky due to close quarters. If you have to repair in the hinge area, tack the repair in place and use the top as a jig to ensure correct positioning.

Sunroofs seldom need repair, but they should be checked for proper operation prior to paint. There are three approaches to installing a sunroof clip. They are documented in the *Restoration Guide*. The approach we use is the one where you only cut out the sunroof section, not the whole roof or roof and window posts.

The metal repair is just about done. One final step is to check for extra holes in the body. Someone may have drilled holes for a front license plate. This would not be

correct and would need to be filled. There may be extra holes in the back panel.

Once we forgot that a customer was going to reposition his side mirror from the door to the fender. We had the 356 painted with the mirror holes still in the door. We had to weld the holes and repaint the door.

That about wraps up the typical metal repairs on the 356. If you have more extensive repairs required by collision or rust damage, you may want to assess whether it is worth doing, particularly if the 356 is a coupe.

Extensive repairs would involve cutting off and replacing major body panels. This is called clipping or installing a clip. Examples would be a complete front or rear clip or a fender or quarter panel. These panels are available and new remanufactured panels can be expensive. Panels from a wrecked 356 may be available and should be less expensive. They would have to be media blasted prior to installation.

Whether using new or used replacement panels, the issue is fit. Many, many measurements will have to be taken and it is very helpful to have an undamaged 356 of the same model available to check measurements.

Another extensive repair would be if the 356 has been hit so hard that the chassis is no longer square. The 356 would have to be put on a frame machine and a knowledgeable technician would have to pull the chassis into alignment. When a 356 takes a hard hit, the force travels through the unibody construction. A hard hit in the left front can result in damage at the right rear. Finding a knowledgeable technician to make these repairs may be difficult and expensive.

Many 356s have damage to the left front. This is due to the left turn scenario. If you are making a left turn and get hit in the front, the left front takes the damage. If you hit someone making a left turn, you take the damage to the left front. Years ago we bought the remains of front clips from a Porsche body shop that went out of business. Almost all the remains were the right side. The left side of the front clip had been used for a repair.

We restored a 1962 coupe for a young lady. The car had been her father's and she received it when he died. She had driven it all through high school and it was very rusty. It also had left front damage. The damage occurred as her father was driving her mother to the hospital for Abby's birth. They made it in time.

One 356 we restored we referred to as "Frankenstein." This was a 356 that was stripped and abandoned in the Colorado mountains. When the land it was on became public, it was removed on a police tow. The tow guy gave the chassis to his brother. It was a 1960 cabriolet and needed rust repair to every panel. Fortunately, no bullet holes, but since the owner got it for free and it was a cabriolet, it was worth restoring.

We will have to find a repair piece for this rear seat area from a parts car.

There may still be rust repairs necessary on parts removed from the 356. An example would be the dash top. This is another piece with foam rubber under the vinyl. If the sponge gets wet, the dash metal rusts, usually at the ends. The metal dash should be media blasted and then repaired. Replacement metal dashes are not available. Repairs can be made with fiberglass, which is easier than trying to fabricate metal. Use small squares of fiberglass, one piece at a time. The repair will be hidden by the dash cover. Other parts that may need repair are seat rail mounts, pedal cluster, and heater cans.

Sometimes a 356 has been stored outside and rain has collected in the rear seat buckets, causing rust damage. Unfortunately, individual replacement pieces are not available. You will have to patch or fabricate a repair piece. There are wire bundle clamps for the starter and rear electrics wiring harness under the seats. Ensure the wire harnesses are pulled away prior to repair.

In 1963, the owner of a '61 Roadster spun the 356 on a wet road in Texas and into a bridge abutment. He was killed. The impact was at the driver side door. A local mechanic bought the wreck to remove and use the transmission. The 356 sat in a field until 1998. They even used it to feed horses. The mechanic's son, who

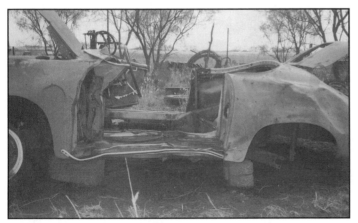

The '61 Roadster mentioned above. You can see the transmission was removed. The Roadster was stored outside in West Texas for 35 years. When straightened on the frame machine, the dent in the left rear fender disappeared.

We can make a repair piece for this damage. We will have to remove the tarpaper insulation.

wasn't even born when the accident occurred, heard about our shop and sent us pictures of the wrecked 356. He wanted to know if it was repairable. We indicated if we could get it square on a frame machine, it was possible. If not, he would be out the expense of the frame machine time.

The Roadster was trailered to Colorado, and we took it to the only frame machine in town set up to do a 356. The day we took it to the shop, a guy came to the shop looking for work. He was the guy that used the frame machine for extensive repairs to 356s at the dealership in the early days! With his expertise, the '61 Roadster was made square and was restored.

The collision impact was at the driver's door. A section from a donor 356 was obtained including front hinge post, rear lock post, threshold, rocker, and longitudinal. Using a Roadster door as a jig, the complete section was welded in place.

Chapter 5

Paint Preparation

Tools used in this chapter are indicated as used.

Gaps

The first step to get the 356 ready for the painter is to use fillers to create the proper gaps around the doors, hood and rear lid just like the factory did. A 3.5 mm gap prior to paint is about the thickness of a wooden paint stirring stick. Use a paint stick to check gaps. The 3.5 mm gap anticipates the addition of primer and paint.

Fillers

The factory used lead to create uniform gaps and to finish seams and correct imperfections. To do the gap at the front and rear of the door, they would fill the opening with lead and run a special tool the length of the opening to create the 3.5 mm gap. While we learned leading skills and have used lead in the past, more and more we are using today's polyester resin fillers. To use lead, the area must be absolutely clean prior to tinning.

Tinning is the process of adding a flux to the surface to get the lead to adhere. A good tinning flux is 95-5 tin-antimony flux in a paste form. Powdered flux does not work as well. The paste is applied to the area with a small brush and then heated with a propane torch. It is quickly wiped with a clean rag and a shiny silver tinned surface will appear.

The tip of a lead stick with 30% tin is then heated until the lead drops onto the tinned surface. Quickly, a wooden paddle which has been saturated with oil is used to spread the lead over the tinned surface. After the lead has hardened, it can be worked with body files to the proper contour. If lead is applied to an untinned area, paint solvents can get under the lead and cause lifting or bubbles in the paint. This is why we now use polyester resin fillers. Now you can buy a gallon of filler for $10 or $30. Guess which one shrinks. A good quality filler is applied to clean metal. Use metal prep, a phosphoric acid product, to clean the

area, rinse and dry. Lightly sand the area with 80 grit sandpaper. Read and follow the directions on your filler can. Do not mix more hardener than recommended. When mixing, fold, don't stir, the filler and hardener to color consistency. *We use a craft stick to initially mix the filler then fold with the spatula.* Use special metal or plastic spatulas to apply filler; these and a plastic mixing board are available at auto paint stores.

Years ago, we sent a 356 out for paint. We watched the shop help mix filler. They really stirred it. We didn't know this was incorrect. Weeks after the 356 had been painted, you could see the pinholes develop as the air bubbles in the fillers collapsed as the paint hardened.

Examples of fillers discussed in the text.

If you are going to use filler on an area and expect it to be between one-sixteenth and one-eighth of an inch thick, use a filler reinforced with fiberglass strands. For the door and lock post edges, use an all-metal filler. This product, which is an aluminum polyester filler, appears like lead when finished. It mixes differently than polyester resin fillers, so read the directions. All these products – metal prep, polyester filler, filler with fiberglass and all-metal – are available from automotive paint supply stores. Ask for the tech sheets on all products.

As you apply filler, it is best to apply it in multiple thin layers. A thick layer can fail due to uneven curing. Also, since you only have a few minutes to apply before hardening, it helps to have multiple areas prepped and ready for filler. Clean the area, then lightly sand. You will want to fill in the darker lower areas. Circle with a pencil. Mix your filler and fill these areas. Mix another quantity of filler and fill another area while the first hardens. Filled areas will be ready for sanding in 20 minutes. A rasping tool, often called a *cheese grater* can be used to remove excess filler before it hardens. Prior to the next layer of filler, clean the area with a light blow of air.

When working filler around the hood and rear lid, reinstall the latches to keep them flush. When reinstalling the hood latch, it may not line up due to repair. First remove a vertical inspection plate (if it is present), the one with the bulge. This is for access in case the hood jams shut. Install

The dual action (DA) sander is in front of the flat sander. A couple of *cheese graters* are also shown.

If the 356 has an inspection plate cover it is a good idea to remove it when adjusting the hood latch. This will provide access if the hood jams shut.

a safety wire from the female latch to an opening in the left side inner fender panel. Attach the male latch to the hood using your scribe marks. Place masking tape over the opening in the female latch. Gently close, but not shut, the hood. Check that the male latch has made a mark in the center of the opening. If so, remove the tape and shut hood.

If the latch mark was off center or the hood didn't shut flush, you will have to remove and disassemble the male latch to be able to adjust it. You want to be able to rotate or shorten the pin so it hits the center of your tape. Sometimes this is an easy job; sometimes it can take most of the day to get the hood to latch properly.

You can use an air powered flat sander or dual action (DA) sander for initial sanding with 40 grit sandpaper. Sandpaper comes with adhesive or Velcro backing to fit on your sander. After 40 grit, you can move to 80 grit attached to wooden sanding blocks. They come in various sizes. You can see low spots in your filler area as they are darker. If you see metal, stop. You have hit a high spot and it must

be dressed down before proceeding. To do this, use a nail set and lightly tap around the outside edges working inward. When lowered, fill the area and move on. When you think you have an area flat, lightly spray with a dark color spray paint. Let dry and sand with 80 grit paper on your sanding block. The dark areas are low areas that need to be filled.

Since the door latch and striker plate are installed, the door can remain shut while you get it flush and with proper gaps. The door should be close to flush as you used it as a jig when doing repairs to the fender in front of the door and quarter panel behind the door. Use a straightedge to determine the area on either side of the door gap that will need filler to make the door flush. To get the proper door gap, it just makes sense to do it like the factory. First ensure your bottom door gap is even. Since no filler is used to create this gap, it should be a tight gap of approximately 1 mm. Spread a wide strip of filler over the front door gap and on both sides and wait with utility knife in hand. Don't mix more filler or take a phone call. As the filler hardens, test with your knife until the filler is easy to cut on both sides of the door gap. Open the door and remove the excess filler. It is obvious what will happen if you wait too long. You will have to use a rotary tool to cut the hardened filler to open the door.

If you have replaced the lock post, you can get those crisp edges using the All-Metal product. This will be stronger than the polyester fillers and less prone to chipping. It helps if you have another 356 available or pictures to get these edges correct. The edges disappear as they get to the top of the lock post.

Use the above procedures to do the filler work, including gaps on all areas of the exterior. This is hard, dirty work. Filler dust will get everywhere. Use of air tools will spread the dust everywhere. Wear your respirator and sweep up often. So far only 80 grit sanding has been done to achieve a rough finish. The painter will do the finish sanding. When the hood is latched and the gaps correct, you can re-drill the index holes. Use a drill bit the same size as the original index hole on the hinge and drill through the original index hole creating a new hole in the hood bracket. Fill the old hole in the hood bracket with two-part putty.

Stringing a 356. On this cabriolet we have used a cloth measuring tape to check the body every inch. If there is a gap between the string and body there is a low spot or adjacent high spot.

One technique to ensure that the 356 is straight is called stringing. Mark one inch horizontal lines at the front of the front fender and rear of the rear fender. With the doors on and latched, stretch a string on each one inch line from front to rear. Other than a slight depression at the door gaps, the string should touch the body evenly. If it doesn't, you need more filler in that area.

Marking a low spot for filler.

Finishing

Before taking the 356 to the painter, it will be necessary to finish the bottom, front compartment, interior and engine compartment. The finish on the bottom of the car will be a rubberized undercoat.

To prepare the underside of the 356, clean all areas except suspension and transmission with metal prep using a green scratch pad. The acid will clean and the scratch pad will give the surface the *tooth* we need for paint. This is a

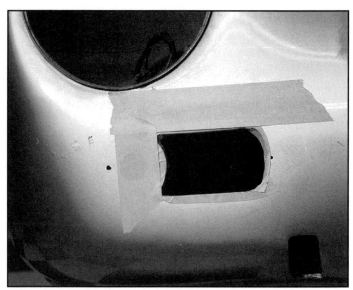

It is important to mask off ledge areas to protect the exterior finish from paint and undercoat applied underneath.

messy job. Wear eye protection and rubber gloves. Follow the directions. Do an area, let it set for a few minutes, then rinse with water. Dry with towels or air and then hit the seams with your propane torch to ensure the moisture is gone. When all the metal surfaces are clean and dry, we are ready for two-part epoxy paint.

You must mask off all exterior openings and holes. Carefully mask off the horn grille openings and torsion hole openings, and rear exhaust openings that have ledges. You are going to need a drop cloth under the 356. It will stay there until after undercoat. So you may want to put the wheels on, take the 356 off the jack stands, position the drop cloth and get the 356 back up in the air. Paint all the underside with two-part epoxy paint. You don't need an expensive spray gun for this application. Wear old clothes, a respirator and rubber gloves. Have a 500-watt lamp handy. Mask off the shocks with aluminum foil, put plastic bags over the brake drums/discs, and protect brake lines. All the wires should still have their protection that we put on prior to media blasting. If the transmission is not too dirty, you will want to protect it. Get some fans going and paint away.

After the paint is dry, caulking is next. *We use 3M All-Around Autobody Sealant Part number 08500.* This is a water-based product while other caulks are solvent based. With this 3M caulk and caulk gun, you can work it into seams with a wet finger. You can also use it on the sides of a rough weld to feather into the area. You should caulk all seams and all areas where rust had developed, i.e. the mud traps:

- All seams
- Fender brace attachment to outer skin
- Around fog light bracket
- Around pedal cluster bracket
- Around headlight bucket
- Around shock absorber mounts

Turn the top of the front closing panel from flat to a sloped surface by applying half a tube of caulk.

- Back of front struts
- Back of diagonal, keeping drain hole open
- Front closing panel to skin
- Lock post to skin
- Bottom inner door seam, but paint first

At the top of the front closing panel, use one half tube of caulk and change the ledge into a sloped surface. After the caulk dries, paint the caulked areas with two-part epoxy paint.

We restored a 1961 D'Ieteren Roadster. No collision damage, minimal rust damage. One area that needed repair was the battery box floor. We saw heavy caulk in the floor seams, one quarter to one half inch wide. We had never seen this before. It must have been done by a previous owner. But further checking revealed all the seams on the Roadster had heavy caulk. It was obviously factory applied and must have been applied wet as you could see sags on some vertical seams. We carefully removed some from the battery box, and it was still pliable after forty years! When we re-caulked the battery box floor after repair, we duplicated the caulk pattern. This 356 had the original floor pan, and we credit this to the use of caulk. While other body builders used some caulk, only D'Ieteren caulked all the seams and did it heavily.

You can use seam sealers prior to caulking, but it is redundant as you have applied two-part primer over bare metal seams. The whole idea is to prevent moisture and air that cause rust in seams.

Undercoat

There are many brands of undercoat and they all must be good as we have never read of problems with today's products. *We use Quick Dry Rubberized Undercoat from Transtar Autobody Technologies, Inc. It's called Tremco. We thin it with lacquer thinner about 10% to get a small pebbly pattern. We apply it with an undercoat gun. The undercoat gun attaches to a quart can. So buy four quarts or if you get a gallon can also get a quart can. A gallon of thinned undercoat will do the bottom of a 356. Undercoat has to be mixed well before use. It likes to separate. This is another messy job. Wear old coveralls that you save for this purpose. Wear rubber gloves and protect your hair (if you have some left).*

Do the middle of the floor pan first and work outward. Do the battery box bottom and under the fenders. Do a little extra on the front closing panel for thicker protection. Get into all tight areas. When finished, clean your gun immediately, before the undercoat sets up. You can now remove all the masking but leave the wires and shocks covered until after paint. In addition to undercoat, you may want to apply some fibrous roofing tar under the front fenders. This will protect your fenders from the *stars* that can occur in the paint when a stone is thrown up by a tire. Only put it in areas where stones can hit; it is not a substitute for good undercoat. Fibrous roofing tar is available at home centers, is cheap, but very messy to apply.

Front Compartment

If your 356 had sound-deadening material in the front compartment, now is the time to repair or replace it. Coupes and cabriolets had the material. Speedsters, Roadsters and Convertible Ds did not. If just a few areas are worn or torn, you can repair the area with tar paper and contact cement. You can blend in the repair by spraying it with undercoating from a spray can. This may give a brown color, but it can be painted later. On 1962-65 356s, there is a thick pad around the gas tank. This material is no longer available. You can get heavy duty jute at an auto upholstery store. This will be a thick, gray material. When patching worn areas, try to get tight seams to the original

An undercoat gun and much used supply can.

Caulking the seams in the battery box. When dry the caulked seam is painted with two part epoxy paint. The bottom of the battery box is then undercoated for additional protection.

material. After installation, spray the gray material with undercoat from a spray can. Now clean all the metal surfaces in the front compartment. Mask off around the hood opening and fuse box on later 356s. Paint the metal with two-part epoxy paint. When dry, caulk the seams of the battery box floor. Paint caulk when dry.

If your 356 had undercoat on the inner side panels, undercoat them and the sides of the battery box. Use the same undercoat you used on the bottom of the car. Undercoat the battery box area on all 356s for additional protection. When dry, spray paint the whole inner compartment with satin black spray paint. Remove your masking and you are done.

Engine Compartment

Do the same procedure for the engine compartment. Repair or replace any sound-deadening material. There are

From bottom to top: hood hinge as removed, hood hinge media blasted, hood hinge masked off and painted.

no seams to caulk and undercoat is not necessary. Clean and paint metal with two-part epoxy paint and then paint the compartment with satin black spray paint.

Interior Compartment

Follow similar procedures for the interior compartment. Clean before painting with two-part epoxy paint. Mask off these areas under the dash that you don't want to paint. It appears the factory painted the completed 356 in color - underneath, all compartments and exterior. The compartments were then painted satin black. The black didn't get completely under the dash area so original color could be visible.

After two-part paint, caulk all floor seams. Let dry and paint. On open 356s, it is a good idea to undercoat the floor pan and rear seat area as additional protection from rain. Finish with satin black spray paint in the interior compartment.
Some later 356s had sound deadening material on the floor. If you removed it for floor pan repair, you can buy a replacement from vendors or make your own out of similar material. The pictures you took would show the installation.

Final Prep For Paint

Now you are just about ready for the painter. If extensive repairs were made to the 356, you should fit headlights, bumpers, taillights, scripts, and soft and hard tops.
You can help the painter by painting the back half of the hood and rear lid hinges. There is a natural break on the hinge that separates the part that is attached to the chassis from the part that is attached to the hood/lid. Mask off the front part. Masking tape and aluminum foil works well. Clean and paint the back half with black two-part epoxy paint. After it dries, you can mask it so the painter can apply body color paint to the front half.

On the aluminum door hinge covers, remove the ID plate(s) from the driver side. Cover the ID plate with masking tape. From the back, use your rotary tool to lightly grind down the peened rivet. Push out the rivet with an awl or ice pick. Don't lose the rivets as replacements are different. Hopefully, it sticks to the masking tape. With the ID plate(s) off and stored, you can remove the paint with paint stripper. Protect your eyes and hands.

You should take the doors, hood, rear lid and bumpers off for the painter. Since you know your door hinge pins fit well, you can put some tape on the top and bottom of the door hinge and some rolls of paper in the hinges on the hinge post. This will keep paint out and save you some filing time after paint. You will also take the torsion hole covers, hood/lid hinges, aluminum door hinge covers, and hood and lid male latches, plus female front latch, (except C model 356) to the painter. Let your painter know you want all the holes in the 356 for script, mirrors, license

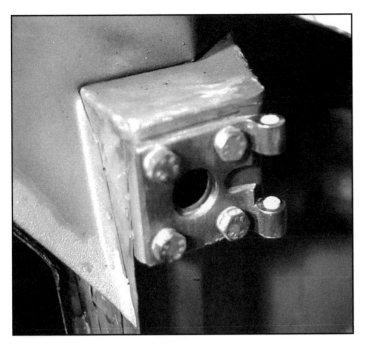
Protecting the hinge prior to paint.

plate, coachbuilder badge, etc., left open. Show him where the holes are.

Painters are usually attached to a particular paint manufacturer i.e. PPG, Du Pont, Glasurit. They must use specified products within the manufacturer's paint system to ensure product warranties. They cannot mix primers, catalysts, reducers, hardeners or paint from various manufacturers.

You will have to provide the painter with a sample of the color you want. Even if you can find an original color formula, you will probably not get the original color as paint products have changed over the years. If you have saved a part with the original color, like a door hinge cover, the painter can have it computer matched at his paint supplier. If you don't have a part with the color you want, the paint supply store will have hundreds of color chips for you to evaluate.

You will have to make a decision on whether to go with a single stage enamel urethane paint or a two stage paint and clear coat. The factory did not use a clear coat and, while it may yield a high gloss, it is more difficult to repair when minor chips occur. Also, it is difficult to find painters and products to duplicate the lacquer paint used on the early 356s.

Also ensure your painter gets enough paint – at least two gallons – and mixes them together. Sometimes the painter may run out of paint and have to get more. If it is not mixed exactly, there will be paint match problems.

While waiting for the painter to do his thing, it is time to clean parts, order replacement parts and order rubber seals. You can also prepare the gas tank, windshields and engine for reassembly.

Cleaning/Ordering Parts

Since you had all your parts bagged and boxed by function and have inspected them during your hardware restoration, you have an idea of what needs to be restored or replaced. Go through each box and bag and separate into needs clean and paint, needs polish, needs replacement. Order your replacement parts from 356 Registry vendors. If a replacement part isn't available from vendors, put it on your internet search list or swap meet needs list.

Most of your rubber seals will probably need replacement. Inventory and order them. Remember to save all rubber parts for patterns.

Many of your parts will just need cleaning and new paint. We recommend the black two-part epoxy paint for hardness, followed by satin black spray paint to duplicate the original look. Some parts will need to be stripped before cleaning and paint. You can box them up and take them to the blast shop or chemically strip them yourself. We usually box the engine tin, bumper brackets, shifter base and seat rail base for the blast shop. Before blasting the engine shroud, try to match the color with a spray paint. Fan shrouds could be black, gray, silver or white. This could have been used to distinguish between normals (black), supers (silver), super 90s (gray), but there are mixed opinions on this. Do not have your oil filler/breather or oil filter can blasted. Material can be trapped inside, come loose later and destroy your engine. Clean these parts by hand.

Fuel Tank

The gas was drained from the tank and a preliminary inspection done prior to disassembly. Now is the time to really evaluate the tank. On early tanks (1950-61), you can see inside with a flashlight to determine if there is varnish buildup from old stored gas. If so, you will want to have the tank cleaned at a radiator shop. On this early tank, you can also place a light bulb inside, turn out the lights and check for pinholes. Obviously, this this should be done only on an early tank that has been dry for quite a while. If you smell gas fumes in the tank, don't do this. If there are many pinholes, you will need a new tank or professional repair. Repairs are very difficult, but you might try a radiator shop. If they repair it, they will want to pressure test it to verify the repair. To do this, they may braze on a fitting. Make sure they do this on the back where it will not be visible when installed.

Don't media blast the early tank, as it has lead covered seams and blasting pock marks the lead. Strip the tank by hand and paint with black two-part primer. Repair any dents, just like you did exterior repairs.

On the later tank (1962-65), first inspect the bottom that has been exposed. If you can see rust damage and pinholes, you will need a new tank or professional repair. You may not see damage now but perhaps after blasting. You can blast the later tank. If the tar paper top cover is in good shape, protect it with duct tape before blasting. Also duct tape the tank openings. If the tar paper top cover is bad, carefully remove it and save for a pattern. Before blasting, though, look carefully at the tank for areas with the original paint. Most of the later tanks are gray, but bottom sender replacement tanks and GT tanks are black. If gray, match the color to a spray paint. You can carry a gas tank into a store to match color.

As mentioned earlier, parts on the 356s were painted 40 to 50 years ago. They were painted with the technology of that day. Even if you have exact paint formulas, you can not exactly duplicate the paint because materials used then may not be available. Plus the color will have changed due to environmental conditions over the years. So the best bet is to get a color match you like and not lose any sleep over it.

So with a gray color match for the tank, send it out for blasting. If pinholes are visible after blasting, try the radiator shop for repairs. For the later gray tank, you will want to prime it with a gray two-part primer. With PPG, this is DP-50. After your early or later tank is in primer, it is time to test the tank.

Fuel Petcock

Your fuel petcock may be ugly with gas varnish. This can be cleaned with lacquer thinner. Replacement parts are available to rebuild the petcock. Replacement petcocks are also available. If you decide to rebuild the fuel petcock, this is covered in the *Restoration Guide*. The rebuild kit will have parts for the different types of petcocks, so note the type and orientation of parts during disassembly. If the petcock is rebuilt or replaced, open the valve and set it in a can of gasoline outside for a few hours to get the inside corks wet.

Testing Tank

It is now time to test the tank and petcock. Install the petcock to your primed tank, making sure the fuel lever connection is to the rear. Note it threads both ways to allow adjustment. Once the petcock is installed, take the tank outside and place on saw horses. Put a quart or so of gas in the tank, turn the petcock to reserve and catch a little gas in a can to verify the petcock is working.

Turn the petcock off and look for leaks. Place a white paper towel under the tank and let it sit for a while. If no leaks, the tank is ready for installation later. Drain the gas from the tank by turning off, removing the bottom cup, turning on and collecting the gas in a suitable container. Leave the tank outside until all the gas has evaporated. You can now remove the petcock and paint the tank, knowing all will be well for installation. If your tank leaks, it may be repairable or you may have to replace it. Find a

Fuel petcock installed on T6 tank for testing.

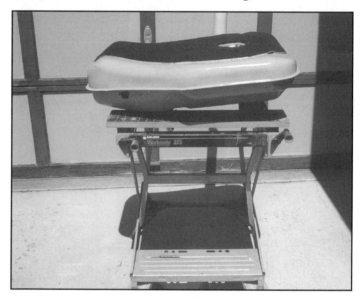

Testing a T6 tank for leaks. No leaks! This was good as two pinholes had to be welded on the tank bottom.

T6 gas tank tarpaper. The grid marks were made by a wire mesh pressed into the tarpaper with a piece of plywood and the family car parked on top.

professional who has repaired fuel tanks and have your tank evaluated.

If you have to replace the tar paper top on your later tank, make two replacement pieces from tar paper using your original pattern. Use contact cement to glue the two pieces together. Note one side of the tar paper has tar on it, which won't allow the contact cement to make a good bond. Use the paper side to cement. Make the top piece just a little bigger to get a nice overlap seal to the tank.

Windshields

Other parts that can be made ready for later reassembly are the windshields for coupes and cabriolets. Do the rear first, since it is a little easier. Support your windshield on a cardboard box or something similar on a table. Use a piece of tape to make a mark on the windshield for the center of the bottom. Slide over the two small aluminum pieces in the center of the trim. Carefully remove the aluminum trim pieces by peeling the rubber back, trying not to bend them. Mark right and left side so you remember. If there is damage to the earlier non-anodized style, it may be repairable using a file, sandpaper and buffing. Replacements are available. Remove the old rubber seal. Clean the windshield. Note the new rubber seal has a rubber weld. Place this at your bottom center mark with the channel for the trim facing out. Put the seal on the windshield, securing every foot or so with duct tape. The last corner will take some careful pulling to get secured to the windshield.

With the seal on, you are ready to reinstall the trim. Clean and polish with your favorite aluminum polish. Try not to bend it. Remove the duct tape. Place the left or right trim piece on the seal with the corners positioned. Note that you are trying to get the hook on the bottom of the trim secured in the seal. Start in a corner. Apply a little silicon spray (use a spray tube on the can) into the seal channel. Note: Do not use silicon spray in an area where there are

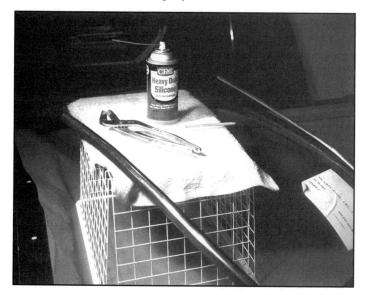

Tools to use to press the deco into the windshield seal.

Some replacement decos have to be trimmed.

parts (or cars) that will be painted. It will cause a fisheye in the paint and the painter will get quite upset. Push the deco into the seal. This is tedious if done by hand. You can make a tool by putting plastic tubing over the jaws of a tongue and groove (slip lock) pliers. Carefully squeeze the deco into the seal. When both decos are in, secure the centers with the small aluminum pieces. Put the rear windshield in a safe place, *storing on edge*. Do the front windshield the same way.

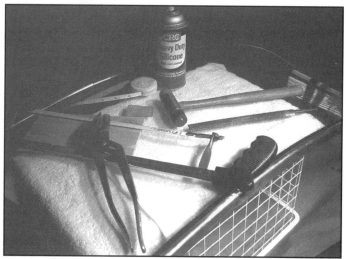

Tools used to install windshield deco. This small wooden wedge and hammer were used to position the center aluminum pieces.

Soft Top Frame

Removal of the soft top frame on Speedsters, Convertible Ds and Roadsters is obvious. Cabriolet soft top removal is more involved as it may have shims at the hinge plate. If the soft top frame needs repair, it should be done before the 356 goes to the painter so you can use the car as a jig. If rivets in the frame have to be replaced, they are available from vendors. One vendor has jigs for open 356 soft tops and can do repairs, paint and recovering of your soft top. If you do the work, you can make repairs, match paint and have the frame ready for recovering at an auto upholstery shop.

Engine

Another big part to get ready is the engine. If your sheet metal is back from the blast shop, you have to decide on paint or powder paint. The factory always used paint; powder paint was not developed until much later. It is a process when a clean part is electrically charged in an oven and the paint powder with opposite charge is applied and melted on to the surface. Some owners prefer powder paint as it is impervious to fuel spills and resists scratches. Since you can't use fillers to repair engine sheet metal prior to powder paint, what you see is what you get. If you want perfect powder painted sheet metal, you have to start with perfect sheet metal.

Note: We understand high temperature fillers are now available. Since we don't powder paint, we have not used them. We use the black two-part epoxy primer on engine sheet metal that has been blasted and cleaned. We don't even paint over the epoxy primer. We have been happy with the original look and have not seen problems with fuel spills or scratches. So it's your call; paint or powder paint.

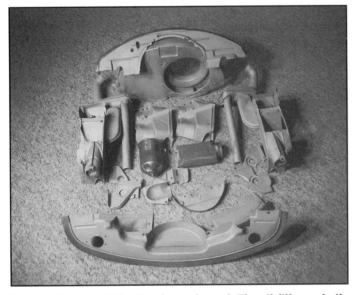

Engine sheet metal that has been cleaned. The oil filler and oil filter canisters were stripped by hand. The other pieces were media blasted.

Other pieces to restore on the engine would be fuel lines, throttle linkage brackets, straps, control rods, oil filter can and generator. Most of the metal pieces are clear (version 1) or silver cad plated. These can be re-plated, but cad platers are hard to find. Zinc plating is similar, or the pieces can be cleaned with very fine steel wool and then painted with a spray can of dull aluminum, followed by a spray can of clear. There were at least a dozen different oil filler cans used over the years, painted different colors and with different decals. You can either replicate what is on your engine or try something different you may have seen on another 356. The generator can usually be cleaned with medium steel wool. The generator brush strap is painted black; the mount strap is cad plated or painted. Your coil could have been black or blue. The blue coil is quite popu-

lar, but black is correct. You can clean the aluminum case with a good detergent and small brushes; dry and rinse with mineral spirits.

Steering Wheel/Knobs

Assuming the plated spokes are good on your plastic steering wheel, you can restore it yourself or send it to a specialist. To do it yourself, mask off the spokes, fill any cracks or deep scratches with filler. Sand with very find sandpaper and paint with the gray two-part primer. Paint to match the original color is available from 356 Registry vendors.

Black knobs for your 1960-65 356 are usually available; the beige, gray and ivory knobs used from 1954-59 are hard to find. If they are finely crazed, you might want to leave

Dipping a fresh air vent knob in lacquer thinner to soften prior to rubbing with a cloth.

them that way for the patina. The knobs can be restored by dipping in lacquer thinner for 10 to 30 seconds to melt the surface and then rubbing with a lint-free cloth. You can leave a little patina or sand lightly. Since you are in the

Soaking ID tags in the metal prep acid, being careful not to lose the rivet heads.

After buffing with steel wool, the ID tags are sprayed with a clear enamel to prevent corrosion.

dash area, you might want to just clean your instruments and check their function later or send them out for rebuild now. Vendors for rebuilding can be found at the 356 Registry web site.

To clean your aluminum ID tags, soak in metal prep and then buff with fine steel wool. Don't lose your rivets.

We were very busy in the shop and we kept getting interruptions. I was bemoaning that fact and how we can't get any work done when the phone rang. "Jim, can you evaluate my 356?" "What do you have?" "Three Speedsters." Well I went to the guy's house, not too far away, and sure enough he had three Speedsters. One stored inside and two stored outside underneath an open lean to roof. The two outside had been there for 20 years. Both had fiberglass tops and plastic side windows for protection, but both were in poor shape." "What's the story?" I asked. "Well my health is not good and I'd like to get one done." I said, "I'll do one for you in exchange for the other." A handshake deal and he picked the '55 with Rudge knock-off wheels. I got the '56. As we worked on his '55, his health improved as he had been mismedicated. He has become a good friend. More on the Rudge wheels later.

Chapter 6

Reassembly

Tools used in this chapter are those used for disassembly in Chapter 2.

Paint Protection

The first thing you want to do is protect the paint. You can't use a wax for 90 days due to out gassing, but you can use a product such as Meguiars Show Car Glaze No. 7. This is a polish, not a wax. It will protect your new paint from spills and sticky fingers for about two weeks, then reapply. But there is no protection from cats! Now is not the time to have cats around your 356. Even with a car cover, cats have a habit of putting out their claws when jumping off your 356. Solve the cat problem if you have it. One suggestion is to try a sheet of plastic over your car cover.

At this time, you need to have a mind set change. Prior to now, you have used all sorts of sharp pointed tools around the 356. From now on, it is important to approach the painted car very carefully with tools. Mask off any area where a tool could slip and damage paint. Use paint masking tape. Wooden craft sticks will be used to push seals into place. Paint will be removed from holes carefully, so

as not to chip. Realize that the paint could get damaged, but is repairable. After all, when you start driving, you expect a few paint chips.

We had one customer who really wanted a super paint job. While he knew we didn't do concours paint, he wanted the best and would pay for the extra time. Well, we did it and it was a great job. He sent us a letter of thanks and said how he would take a glass of wine out to the garage and just stare at his beauty. Years later we saw him at an event and congratulated him on driving his 356. He said he had not been driving it as he was worried about paint damage. But he washed his 356 at a car wash and scratched the fender with the hose. Since his 356 was no longer a "virgin," he drove it all the time. And with a big smile on his face.

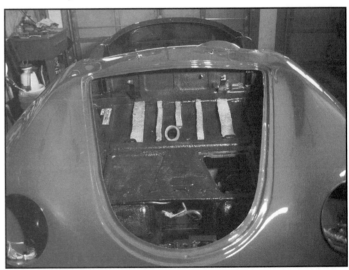

The painted front compartment ready to glue the gas tank insulation pieces. The round piece is the rubber gasket for the fuel petcock opening.

Overspray

Now, mask off the 356 and use spray paint to cover the painter's overspray under the car and to seal the undercoat. Spend the time to mask off all the 356 to protect the

Masking off to front compartment prior to spray paint.

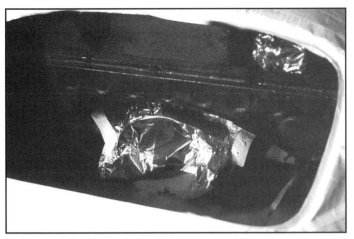

Engine compartment masked and painted. Since this is a Roadster, there is no engine compartment insulation.

Masking off prior to spray painting underside. Mask off ledges of openings.

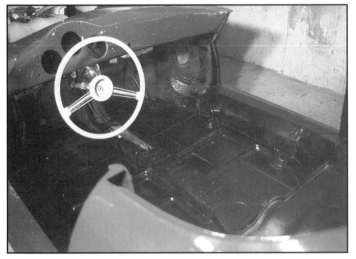

Interior compartment painted.

Ready to spray paint the undercoat.

new paint. Put the car up on jack stands. Pick a slightly different spot this time so you can paint the small areas where the jack stands were when you painted and undercoated before. When masking, pay particular attention to the bottom edge. You want a clear demarcation between the bottom paint and body color. If there is any bare metal here, either missed by you or the painter, hand paint it with two-part primer. Use light stick masking tape available at paint supply stores. Once masked, spray all the undercoat with satin black spray paint.

Cleaning Suspension/Transmission

With the 356 up in the air, it is finally time to clean the suspension and transmission. There are no tricks here, just elbow grease. This job was saved until last to keep overspray from previous work from getting on a cleaned area. After cleaning and since the car is up in the air, the 356 should be lubed. Lubrication points are specified in your owners manual in detail with pictures.

Cleaning Brake Drums/Backing Plates

To clean brake drums, it is best to remove them. First, back off the brake shoes. Check your workshop manual for the

procedure and direction to turn the adjustment wheels. Since the rear axle nuts were loosened earlier, removal should be straightforward at the rear. At the front, you will have either a hex key/retaining ring or two nuts with a keeper. For the two nuts, tap back the keeper and remove the nuts with a 27 mm wrench or socket. Note that the threads on the left side are reversed.

You can clean the brake drums by hand or have them blasted. Remember there are 72 notches to clean on the 1960-63 drums. Blasting is a lot quicker, but you need to remove or protect oil bearings, races and seals. This is a good time for replacing them anyway.

If you want to remove the backing plates for cleaning or paint, the fronts are secured by special bolts with holes in the head for a safety wire. Note the location of the bolts as one may be shorter to clear the suspension. At the rear, you will be dealing with seals, washers and transmission fluid. You may want to clean or paint the rear backing plates in place. If you want to remove them, use your workshop manual to ensure correct removal and reinstallation. If you are not confident of your mechanical skills when working with safety issues such as brakes, find a professional.

Shock Removal/Painting

The shocks have been on the car all through this process. Now would be the time to remove and evaluate them for restoration or replacement. Removal can be difficult. Notice that at the bottom, where they attach to the stud, there is a rubber buffer and a steel bushing. This bushing has a tendency to rust itself to the stud. Apply plenty of penetrating oil to this area and wait overnight. On the front shock, you will have to jack up the suspension to take the load off the top bolt. On the rear, loosening the top nut will sometimes cause the top half of the shock to spin. Secure this with a strap clamp, if needed.

With the top of the shock disconnected and the bottom nut and washer off, move the shock to see if the bottom bushing in the rubber buffer will move. If so, pry off the shock. If not, try to get it to move with pry tools, hammer work and penetrating oil. If the rubber buffer comes off and the bushing is still rusted to the stud, try heat, pipe wrench, whatever. There is a technique in the *Restoration Guide* to get this bushing back in the rubber buffer. If it doesn't come off, you will have to replace the bushing or the shock. Remove the bushing by cutting it with the side cutter, splitting it and prying off.

If the shock is removed successfully, test it by pulling and compressing in a vertical position. If it feels correct i.e. goes down easy, comes up hard, clean it, paint it and reinstall. If you have to replace shocks, there are some specifications in the *Restoration Guide*. Today, you can spend from $20 to $100 or more per shock. Since this item, like tires, is variable due to personal preference and driving style, you should select a replacement shock absorber that suits your needs. There is a product called Never Seeze that should be used on metal to metal connections like the shock bushing to stud connection. It will keep these parts lubricated and facilitate future removal.

There is also a shock absorber up front called the steering dampener. Remove it and test it in the horizontal position. If okay, clean, paint and reinstall. If it feels faulty, replacements are available but some may not be of the correct length. Check before installing.

Where to Start?

You can start reassembly with the exterior, the interior compartment, the engine compartment or the front compartment. If you are replacing the wiring harness, now would be the time. There are several vendors for 356 wiring harnesses. Replacement harnesses are expensive, but come with excellent instructions for installation. Also when reinstalling electrical components, they should be bench tested first. Use your battery or battery charger. It's nice to know a horn or light assembly works before installation.

Front Lights

The 356 looks much better with its eyes. If you are using your original headlights, which you may have restored with new chrome or polished rim, new glass and painted interior, they should drop right in. Use new rubber seals between the headlights and body. If you are using a reproduction headlight assembly, it may not fit without some dressing of the bucket edge. Hopefully, you found and corrected this during restoration or dry fit. Dressing this area means pulling in the bucket edge to fit the assembly. This will cause the paint to chip, which you must touch up after you achieve fit.

When installing the front turn signals in the 1960-65 356s, you may have to cut notches in the profile to get it to bend. Your original can serve as a pattern. If the profile is flexible enough, you can try it without notches. Also of note, the wire to the turn signal light doesn't go through

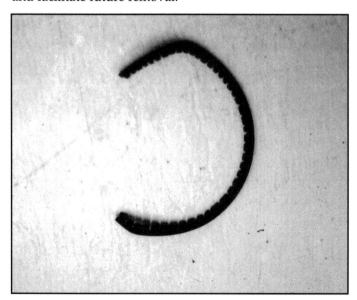

Rubber profile that goes under the T-5, T-6 front turn signal. This original piece was notched to make the curve around the turn signal.

If the rubber turn signal profile is flexible sometimes it can be applied without notches having to be cut. It helps to have someone hold the turn signal and profile tight to the body as the unit is secured from behind.

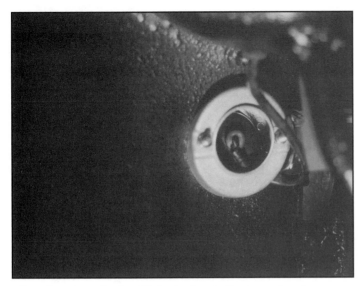

The wires from the headlight bucket to the turn signal go under a notch in the backing plate. This also makes installation easier than running the wires through the center of the backing plate.

the center of the backing plate but goes under the smaller notch in the backing plate. The larger notch is a drain.

Front Compartment

Do the front compartment next. For the early 356, attach the ID tag or tags to the bottom side of the gas tank location. The original rivets should still be taped to the ID tag. Dry fit to see if the rivets will stay in the holes. Enlarge the holes slightly with an awl if needed. When it fits, glue down with two-part 5-minute cement at the rivet holes. Place a weight on top until set. For the later 356, the ID tags in the center of the front compartment can be pop riveted into place. On 1962-65 356s, install the fresh air vents on both sides. If you decide to repaint them, mask off the metal attachment parts. The vent cover grilles can be painted dull aluminum. You will probably need a silicone spray to work the vents into the rubber receivers. Secure under fender with washer and nut. You can now install the front hood hinges.

Gas Tank

Now, install the gas tank. Reinstall the fuel petcock in the proper orientation. For the 1953-61 tank, there was a cloth material between the straps and tank. If yours is not reusable, a gray or brown felt material can be found at a fabric store. There is also material on the ribs under the tank. Installing the early tank is straightforward. There is a rubber seal between the tank and petcock opening.

Once that tank is in, you should take the time to connect the tank to the tunnel fuel line. It is embarrassing later if you fill the tank and have forgotten this connection. Put a shop rag at the end of the tunnel line with rubber bands and blow out the line. Hopefully, there is little crud on the towel as you have protected the fuel line since before media blasting. If there is crud, you need to flush the tube

with a solvent, i.e. lacquer thinner. Do not have a light under the car when blowing out or flushing the gas line.

For fuel lines, you can use German 7 mm line available from vendors or five-sixteenths rubber fuel line available at auto parts stores. The five-sixteenths line will need hose clamps, but it doesn't deteriorate as fast as the 7 mm line. Plan to inspect 7 mm fuel lines yearly. The 7 mm line doesn't need clamps, but they are recommended.

Installation of the 1962-65 tank is more complex as learned during disassembly. No tricks here. Installation is the reverse of disassembly. However, you may want to check the vent tube at the top right of the tank. Run a wire in the tube to make sure it is clear.
On the 1962-65 356s, you can now install the fresh air drain box if present. The washer bottle and fuse cover can be installed. If you need new rubber straps, they can be made from an inner tube.

Hood Seal

To attach the hood seal, you start in the upper right hinge area, but first clean the seal. *We use 3M Liquid Adhesive Remover. This is an excellent product for cleaning rubber and other parts, not as aggressive as lacquer thinner and more effective.* There are four holes for the hood seal corner piece screws. Between the two lower screw holes, you should see a factory weld across the hood channel. This is your starting point. Others have reported the starting point between the two middle screw holes or between the last two screw holes. You can use the seal you removed to determine your start point as long as it was in the right corner. The seals on real early 356s are described in the *Restoration Guide*. Before installing the hood seal, check it for length then tape each side and lightly sand. This will allow for a glue bond later. Start the seal with the tip of the V pointed inside and the wider part of the V on top.

The hood seal at the starting point. The dirty paper towel is from cleaning the hood seal. It has to be clean for the glue to work later.

The hood seal has been installed around the sides and has been trimmed with a new razor blade.

Your corner piece should be black; if not, paint with two-part black primer. Orient your corner piece to the screw holes. Place the corner seal in the crease of the V. Line up the end of the seal with the factory weld and secure to the lower screw hole. A finish washer is not used on this screw. Continue to the next lower screw hole; use an ice pick to puncture the seal over the hole and secure with a screw and finish washer. Continue around the hood opening to the left side upper corner. Do not stretch the seal. At the left corner, you bend, not cut, the seal to make the curve and insert the corner piece and secure without finish washers. Continue over to the right corner. Make the curve and mark for your end cut. Make the mark a little long. You want to get a very tight end-to-end joint. Make your cut, slip the end under the corner piece and check the joint. Trim as necessary and secure with screws. Remember to use a new blade in your utility knife.

Once the hood seal is installed, remove a screw with finish washer, lift up the seal and apply a thin bead of contact cement to the seal and lightly sanded surface. Use craft sticks to keep the seal from touching the paint. Wait the recommended time and glue together.

The hood seal joint. Use of Super Glue to the ends is optional.

If for some reason, the holes in the body for the hood seal have been filled, you sometimes can find them by looking/feeling under the hood seal lip. If not, you can get the location measurements from another 356. There was probably not a factory jig for these holes as they vary in location, but they are usually 17 cm to 19 cm apart on the sides and closer at the front.

Hood Installation

Now install the hood. Do this with the male latch off and hood handle installed. Use your original rubber/plastic seals as patterns for the new seal for the hood handle. On 1960-65 356s, don't forget the two rubber washers. Installation of a painted hood is a two person job; lay towels at the corners for protection. With the hinges up, attach hood to hinge using index holes as reference. The hinge goes inside the hood brackets. Close slowly and carefully. Ensure the back of the hood is not going to touch the rear opening. Move the hood forward if this appears to be the case. With the hood carefully closed, check for proper gap and make very small adjustments to get the gaps perfectly centered.

Temporarily attach the male latch and use masking tape to ensure it is centered on the female latch. Make the adjustments, which were described earlier, as necessary. Make sure the inspection plate is still off and the safety wire is installed. Close and latch the hood. Hopefully, when you release the hood, it pops up. If not, you can get to it through the inspection plate opening. Your hood may sit a little high until the seal sets. You can adjust this after a few months.

Headliner-Coupe and Hardtop

For the interior, start with the headliner. The headliner comes folded and will have creases. There are also extra pieces. These will be used for the pillars, below the quarter windows and behind the rear panel. You can get the creases out of your headliner by using an iron on low heat or a hair dryer. On the roof of the 356 coupe should be two pieces of insulation material. If they came off during disassembly, glue them in place, using the ghost marks from the headliner bows. A spray glue works well. Now insert the bows into the headliner in the order they were removed and marked. Do this carefully so as not to tear the headliner. Place the rubber tips on the bow ends, securing with black tape. Inside the 356, start at the front and secure the bow in the side notches, using the ghost mark on the insulation to position. Secure the other three bows.

Secure the headliner at the front and rear windshield openings. Hold with spring clips or binder clips, i.e. the black ones you get at office supply stores. Now check for position. The area around the rear of the quarter windows is of critical importance and side-to-side is also important. Pull and stretch and reposition your clips until centered. Mark with a pencil the front and rear of the headliner where it meets the windshield opening. Mark the headliner with pencil for the sun visor and mirror hole. Remove the clips at the front. Then apply contact cement to headliner at your pencil marks and openings.

After the recommended time, secure the headliner in front. Do the same in back, pulling tight. Let it sit overnight. The next day, start pulling the sides tight and securing with clips. You want the headliner tight without wrinkles. You can remove a glued section and refresh the glue lightly to reposition. On 356Cs, there is a rear defroster vent on each side. Secure the vent tube to the small pipe in the chassis and clip to the window opening before securing the headliner to this area of the window opening. Continue the repositioning and gluing until you are satisfied. Remember the critical area at the rear of the quarter windows; it has to come down and around the bottom of the window. There is also a lot of extra material that goes behind the rear panel. Pull down on this material to get the area behind the quarter windows tight. As you work behind the quarter windows, you can remove the quarter window latch screws and mark their position on the headliner. When you are satisfied with the installation, you can trim the excess from the window and door openings, and install the original clips. Make sure the headliner is glued tight in these areas or you will have difficulty gluing in seals. If there is any excess glue around the headliner, remove it with the 3M Liquid Adhesive Remover.

For the pillars, use the four pieces provided. Fold over and glue the top about one quarter inch. Clamp and let dry. Position the folded top to the top of the pillar and glue around the pillar. The long wide strip goes below the rear window. The two shorter strips go below the quarter windows. These strips hide the reveal between the window seals and inner panels.

Headliners for sunroofs are similar except you don't have any bows. You get it tight and glued on all four sides and then make your X cut for the opening. When attaching the headliner to the sliding panel, make sure the corners are flush. Do not have headliner material gathered at the corners or the panel will not slide in its channel.

Interior Panels

Next, the carpet, but before it can be installed, the side panels and back panels must be installed. Do the side panels first. The vinyl has some padding and is glued to a weatherboard, which is hard cardboard resistant to moisture. If you are using the originals, there should be a curve in the weatherboard. If using a new panel, you will have to score or wet the board to get it to bend. You may also have to use a sheet metal screw to secure the board to the chassis. The vinyl wraps around the door seal opening. Glue in both side panels.

The coupe back panel can be difficult because the factory used long nail studs to secure it to the firewall, but then cut the studs after installation. The padding that goes behind the panel should still be in place. If you have the defroster tube that goes behind the rear panel (1960-63), you should install it now. Find the holes in the padding. You may have to cut openings in any excess headliner material. Start with the bottom studs and insert them in the holes and into the engine compartment. Secure with small vice grips. Insert the other studs. The studs were secured with Tinnerman clips, either round or with a washer and rectangular clip. You can reuse your original clips by lightly tapping them down with a hammer. If you have trouble securing the rear panel, a trick is to cut four to five inch pieces of small tubing. Insert them through the fire wall and padding, making an easily accessed hole, and use them to align your studs.

Carpet

You can do the carpet yourself and save some money, particularly on coupes. On an open 356, because of their value, it is best to consider an upholstery shop for the professional look. The following is for coupes. Spend the extra money for the German square weave carpet; the domestic just doesn't look right. The only tricky part is at the rear section of the inner longitudinal. You should have your pictures to remind you of what piece is under another piece. You should also have noted where carpet nails were used. The upholstery shops use a spray glue. You can use a spray can glue or contact cement. Start with the forward carpet piece that will become the back of your pocket. Position it and mark the edge of the piece with chalk on the chassis. Apply glue to the carpet piece and to the chassis up to your chalk marks and install. Note that you do not have to glue in the radio speaker area. You do have to glue the vinyl material to the door seal area. Make sure the top of the vinyl is to the bottom of the dash. The next piece is your pocket piece. It was secured with some carpet nails or screws with finish washers to make it tight. Note you shouldn't glue behind the pocket.

Gluing the front pillar piece.

The difficult area of carpet installation. The area is saturated with hot water to make it pliable. All the edges of the carpet are stretched and fit before the cut is made over the vertical panel.

To make progress while waiting for the glue to get tacky, you can alternate sides. The next piece will be for the inner longitudinal. It may be one or two pieces. You want to get it tight to the front door opening and parallel with the threshold edge. Only glue it back about three-fourths of the inner longitudinal and let it set before doing the tricky part. The tricky part is the area at the back of the inner longitudinal where you have to fit some funny angles and stretch to get over the back vertical piece and up the edge of the side panel. To make these bends and curves, use a spray bottle with hot water. Really soak the carpet. The upholstery shops will use a steamer in this area, but they know how to be careful with wool carpet. With the carpet wet, stretch, pull and pound into place before making the necessary cut at the top of the vertical rear seat panel. Apply your glue while the carpet is still damp and when tacky, glue into place. A rubber mallet wrapped with a towel helps to work the carpet down. An alternative is to coat the carpet twice with contact cement and use a heat gun to make the carpet pliable.

The next carpet piece will be the horizontal rear shelf piece. It tucks under the rear panel and drops down in the rear seat area. Early 356s (1953-59) may have a vinyl piece that drops down. This is fairly easy to glue in place. On later 356s (1960-65), the next piece is the hump piece. The horsehair padding should be in place on the chassis. Saturate the piece with hot water to form on the hump. Make as few relief cuts as possible. When formed, glue into place. Next is the vertical piece in front of the rear seat. You should apply some padding at the top of this panel. Otherwise, when you bend the carpet over the top, the carpet base fabric will show. It seems today's carpet doesn't have as many loops per square inch as the original carpet. Do the tunnel access cover next; hot water will help. The tunnel cover that goes under or around the seat rails is straightforward to apply.

The weatherboard piece on later seat backs; it keeps the carpet from dropping into the area behind the seat.

Last will be the carpet on the seat backs. Early 356s (1953-59) have one piece, glued and tacked into place, sometimes sewn on the corners. Later cars with split rear seats have two pieces glued and tacked into place on each seat back. They also have a piece of weatherboard secured to the seat that slides to keep the carpet from dropping into the crack. They are also secured by screws and finish washers onto small raised platforms below the rear panel. Now, go back and cut out the hole for the heater slides on the inner longitudinal. Pull up the carpet in this area to find the hole, mark with chalk and cut. If you did not do metal work in this area, find the holes for the header slides and mark, using an ice pick through the carpet. Glue the carpet back in place and secure the heater slide. If you have to drill new holes for the heater slide, cut a small x where you will drill so your bit doesn't catch a thread and unravel the carpet. You can also use a sharp ice pick to make the hole by hitting through carpet and inner longitudinal.

Threshold

With the carpet in, you can secure it with the aluminum trim on the threshold. But while there, you might as well do the bottom door seal and threshold rubber as well. It is best if you can restore the original aluminum trim at the door opening. The reproduction pieces often do not line up with the original screw holes in the chassis. If you use a reproduction, use your original to cut the reproduction to length. Mark screw holes and drill with the proper size bit as determined by an original hole. For the carpet trim, you will be drilling through three layers of metal.

Next will be the threshold rubber; use your original as a pattern, noting the notches at the ends and wide ridge on the outside. Glue in place. Now install the aluminum trim rail, which captures the edge of the threshold rubber. Once again, you may have to drill new holes. Before drilling, protect the paint on the rocker with tape! Use new bits to drill holes. You can size the drill bit by drilling into a spare sheet metal piece and trying the screw. Some of the screws provided in kits are soft and will break off if the hole is too small. The final piece is the lower door seal with U channel. If the U channel is not painted, paint with two-part black primer. Use your original threshold seal or use it as a pattern for the replacement. The U channel sits inside the threshold seal and is secured by four slotted screws. If you have to re-drill these holes, push the seal and U channel as far into the threshold opening as possible and drill at an angle.

Dash

Since you took good notes during disassembly, assembling the dash should be straightforward. Start at the top and then work left to right. Use your notes or the great books from 356 Electrics to guide your instrument connections. The first part to install would be the windshield washer nozzles. You may have to cut back some of the tubing to get a tight connection. The brackets that secure the instruments also act as a ground. If you painted behind the dash, use sandpaper to re-establish a ground. One part that can be frustrating is the glove box: lining up the screws with the bracket. The screws are long so that you can catch a few threads at the top, then push back the glove box to see and line up the bottom screw with the bracket.

The glove box screws are long to ease installation; just catch a few threads at the top so you can see the nut on the strap to engage the lower screw. This 356 has an optional inside/outside thermometer in the clock position and the clock moved to the right of the glove box, as shown in the workshop manual. It also has a swiveling map light that illuminates when moved from the down position.

In the battery story, I mentioned the special two fuse block for the electric sunroof. It is located under the dash on the bulkhead near the turn signal flasher. The second fuse is used for the optional electric radio antenna.

Doors

Before hanging the doors, re-attach the wedge shaped

Masking off the door area when installing the door is important because the door gap when opening and closing the door is very tight.

doorstops that attach to the front closing panel. Your originals are probably worn but may work with a wooden shim. New ones are best as the originals get too hard. Slide them to the outer edge of the elongated hole. Washers and nuts go on the closing panel. Also ensure the lower doorstop buffer is secured to the door. Your original is probably reusable; you may have left it on and covered with tape. Also remove the tape over the hinge pin openings on the hinges. If there is any tape residue, remove with 3M Liquid Adhesive Remover.

Now for the doors. It is easier to hang the doors and then reassemble. If you assemble the doors off of the car, they will be heavier to hang and you run the risk of paint damage while working on a workbench. Mask off the front door opening and the front of the door. Have your milk crate in position, covered with a towel. Have your hinge pins and hammer close by. Put a little oil on the hinges. Carefully insert the door into the opening. Insert top pin, then bottom; tap into place. Very slowly, start to close the door, looking for possible contact areas. If the masking tape starts to touch, open the door, remove the tape and slowly close again. If it looks like the door is going to touch, open it and adjust the hinges back just a bit. When the door shuts without touching, reinstall the latch, opening mechanism and exterior door handle. You can also reinstall the striker plate to keep the door closed.

To reassemble the door, it is the reverse of disassembly, as the workshop manual indicates, but here is a little more elaboration. First fit the top chrome piece and profile. Use a new profile. Use tape to hold the chrome piece and profile in place. Use a new fuzzy strip, cut to length using your old one as a pattern. Use an awl or ice pick to punch holes in the fuzzy strip to line up with holes in the chrome piece. Bury the screw heads in the fuzzy strip and attach it and the chrome piece to the door. Some 356s may have had cardboard shims to properly fit the chrome piece to the door. Slide a new window seal into the slot on top of the chrome piece. Do not trim until relaxed, i.e. you don't want it to shrink back. Early 356s have a special window seal with a wire.

Next, install the window regulator, noting the bolt and washer placement from your notes. Clean the glass, place in the door and secure to the regulator. Before installing the window frame, install a new window channel. Note that the rear and top are flexible and the front is steel backed. Glue the new channel to the frame. If you removed the vent window pieces for chroming, they can be reattached to the vent window glass with two-part epoxy cement. Use the pivot point and latch to properly position the pieces in the opening.

Insert the window frame into the door, raising the glass to stay in the window channel. The frame may hit the latch on the way down; just pull the frame away from the latch. With the frame installed, secure it and the brackets with the bolts/washers/nuts noted during disassembly.

If you have had your exterior door handle chromed, you may have to do some filing to get it to fit due to chrome build up and the tight hole opening. First, use some sandpaper on a dowel to clear the handle hole opening. Also carefully clear the opening for the screw hole. Make sure there is no filler inside the door around the openings. With a file, back file the lip area of the handle. With new chrome and a new rubber seal, this area will be too tight to install without some back filing. Continue to file and test until the lip slides into the rear of the large opening. Mask off the area to avoid damage and use a little silicone spray. Use a wood craft stick if you need to reposition the rubber seals.

Installation of the window channels for the Roadster/Convertible D is different. They do not require the channel material. There are little plastic pieces that provide the slide against the aluminum channel. Place the front channel in the front of the door but do not secure it. Secure the rear channel. Attach glass to the regulator and place in rear channel. Now you can secure the front channel to the glass and secure the channel. Note the special adjusting screws to position the glass later, after the top is secured.

Now it is time for the seals that are glued to the front and rear inner door. Use your old seals as patterns. Run them a little long at the top and trim after the door panel and garnish rail are installed.

Mark the holes behind the door seals with an ice pick and chalk mark to make installation of the door panel easier. Install the door panel with new screws and finish washers. Note that there may be a screw and finish washer at the bend of the front door seal. Put a new fuzzy strip on your garnish rail, reusing the clips from your old fuzzy strip. Install your garnish rail, using an ice pick to locate the screw hole and using the longer screws with finish wash-

ers. Install the interior door handle and window crank, using the pictures in the *Authenticity* book for correct orientation

Now install the seals in the door opening. Again, use your old seals as a pattern. Note that on coupes there are little tabs in the door-opening channel. Bend these back and then forward after the seal is glued in place. Dry fit the seal first. On early 356s, you may have to make a cut at the right angle upper corner. Clean the seal and glue in place. Shut the door to hold the seal until glue sets. You will have to pull back and re-glue a section of the seal when you install the dash top.

Windshields

Now install the windshields; start with the rear. The windshields are ready to go since you prepped them while waiting for the painter. Get a length of sash cord about six feet long, the kind used to open/close window blinds. Rub the cord with beeswax. Start with the middle of the cord and place it in the bottom innermost channel of the rear windshield rubber seal. Push in with a craft stick and run up both sides to the top. At the top, cross over the cord about six inches.

Starting on the windshield installation and working to the right side.

If you have a 356C with the two defroster vents, now is the time to install the plastic covers. They clip on the window opening. Don't forget to cut a slot in the headliner material for the vent. Also, put some tape where the plastic vent clips to the window opening. This will keep your cord from hanging up when installing the rear windows. Place the rear window in the opening with the cord ends inside the 356. Center and push down on the rubber seal, getting it to seal as much as possible. Now you need a friend.

With you in the car and your friend outside with his/her palm pushing the windshield in, pull the cord, which will cause the rubber seal to come in and over the lip in the windshield opening. Pull the cord parallel to the wind-

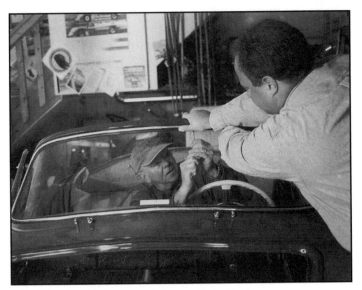

With the right side in, working to the left.

shield. Your friend will push as you pull the cord around and to the bottom. Stop in the middle at the bottom. Go to the top and do the other side. Pull cord out at the bottom and you're done. One of the problems that can occur is having the cord start to cut into the rubber. This would be caused by not enough beeswax on the cord. Stop if this starts to happen and slowly work around the problem. Some installers recommend soapy water for the installation, but too much can cause the windshield to slide in the opening. With the rear windshield in, use the same procedure on the front. If your 356 was painted a light color, i.e. ivory and your interior a dark color, i.e. red, the factory would paint the area between the front of the dash and lower windshield frame the color of the dash top. This would stop reflections on the windshield from the light body color. You can match the color of the dash and paint with a brush. The cabriolet windshield is installed the same as the coupe except you have the mirror rod to install.

Speedsters, Roadsters and Convertible Ds are different. The dash material must be glued in place. You attach the top and side posts of the windshield frame together but leave the machine screws a little loose. Make sure no screw penetrates past the edge of the frame. If it does, you've got the wrong screw and you will crack your windshield. A new seal is installed on the windshield; use your original for length. Using a silicone spray, push the windshield and seal into the frame. Trim the bottom seal to the length of your original and install on the windshield. Mask off the area where the windshield posts go into the chassis. Clean out the post hole with sandpaper on a stick or rat-tail file. On Roadster/Convertible Ds, place the bottom post seal on the posts. Speedsters use a profile rather than a post seal. It must be notched to fit around the post. With a friend, place the posts into the chassis holes and push down, lining up the bottom seal with the bracket on the cowl that will secure the bottom seal and the mirror rod with the opening in the dash. The posts are secured with bolts and washers under the dash.

All this sound easy, but it isn't and will take many tries. On Roadsters/Convertible Ds, it can be more difficult as the windshield glass may have to be trimmed if it is a replacement! There is an excellent article in the *Restoration Guide* including a factory bulletin on Roadster windshield difficulties. Make a paper template from your original Roadster windshield and place on the replacement. If not exact, take the template and replacement to a glass shop to be trimmed. The lower windshield trim on Roadsters and Convertible Ds is very hard to install, particularly if you are using reproduction pieces. The pictures you took before disassembly will be a great help. Do the side pieces first, tucking under the windshield post. Then the center section. The joint between side and center sections is covered by the two clips that go under the rubber seal on the windshield wiper posts.

Now on 1956 and later coupes, you can reinstall your dash top. When removed, you saw how the tabs slide into the slots. So you just need to push it in. At the ends of the dash are little tails of material. They have to go under the door seal. Pull back the seal, set the tails and re-glue. To soften the transition between the dash ends and door seal, parts of cotton balls can be inserted under the dash material. If there was a light in the dash, fish out the wires, install on the light and push the light into the dash. Secure the dash with the screws and finish washers. The interior mirror can be installed now.

Quarter Windows

Move on to the quarter windows. The only trick here is trimming the seals. Since you marked them right and left upon disassembly, you can use the originals to trim the new seals. Note they are cut at the corners and for the latch. The trick cut is for the hinges so the seal slips over the hinge. The seal is not glued. It is oversized and is held in by friction. You may want to glue at the top if it does not fit to the headliner. Installation of the quarter window is straightforward. It helps to use an awl in a hinge hole while securing the machine screw and special nut. With the quarter window in, you can install the rear garnish rail. It has a tab at the rear that slides behind the side of the rear panel. It may clip to a long bracket on the chassis. You should trim the headliner material to expose the bracket. The front is secured by a screw through the door pillar just below the quarter window hinge screw.

With the glass in, finish the interior before starting on the exterior. Install the pedal cluster and accelerator pedal. One caution: some of the replacement toe board mounts for the driver's side come with non-metric captive nuts. If you use a metric bolt to attach the accelerator pedal, you can jam the bolt or spin the captive nut. Then you have to cut out the toe board mounts, repair, re-weld and repaint. With the pedal cluster in, reattach the clutch cable and throttle linkage. Adjust them later. Before installing the shifter, if a later 356, check the condition of the guide ring that the shift rod slides through. If worn or missing, it should be replaced. The shifter can be installed, then the floor boards, tunnel mat and rubber floor mats. Next are the seats and steering wheel. On early 356s, the seat rails on the sides may need to be shimmed with washers to be at the same height as the tunnel rails. Also, if the rails are not wide enough to grip the seat rail, rather than elongating the holes in the seat rail, you can gently bend the seat rail ends in a vise.

When you reinstall the torsion hole covers, cut a circle of headliner material slightly smaller than the cover. This goes between the torsion hole cover and chassis. The factory did this so the paint wouldn't get chipped if the torsion hole cover came loose. Something to check on a concours 356. Also don't over-tighten the torsion hole cover; it could dent. Put a dab of black silicone caulk on all hardware threads exposed underneath the 356 to keep nuts from working loose.

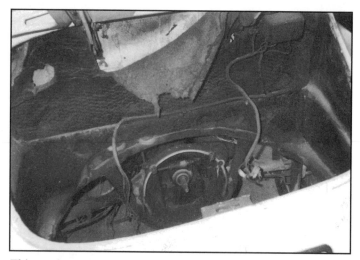

This engine compartment insulation can be repaired by re-gluing and patching with tarpaper. A spray can of undercoat, followed by satin black spray paint, will create a texture similar to the original.

Sound Deadening Material

Coupes and cabriolets have sound deadening material; Speedsters, Convertible Ds and Roadsters do not. The material, which is a heavy tarpaper with a light grid pattern, is glued in the front compartment, engine compartment and in the door hinge post cavity. If you were unable to salvage or repair this material, kits are available. Some are better than others; do some research. A low-cost approach would be to make your own using heavy tarpaper. Contact cement and a heat gun help in installation. Other alternatives are discussed in the *Restoration Guide* on page 350.

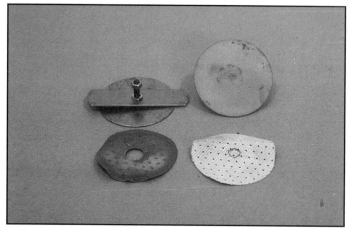

Torsion hole cover headliner gasket. An original is on the left, replacement on the right.

Beltline Side Trim

If you have restored your side trim for an open 356, it should install easily. Due to filler and paint thickness, you may not be able to use your original clips. You can use T-bolts where necessary. These are available from vendors or you can make your own by squaring of the head of an appropriate 4 mm bolt. T-bolts slide into the trim at the ends of the front and rear pieces but not on the door pieces if reusing the original side trim.

The door pieces can be a problem on reproduction side trim as you have to remove the end stops to insert T-bolts. These end stops have to be removed and cut as they are longer than the originals and interfere with fitting. To remove the end stops, note where they have been swedged and carefully drill at these points, just enough to remove the contact area. Secure the trim to your workbench with spring clamps, protect the polished finish and tap out the end stop.

Bumpers

Bumper installation should be straightforward as you fit the deco and dry fit them prior to paint.

Other Parts

To install the sliding panel in your manual sunroof, use the trick of placing in the opening and then installing the side rails. For electric sunroofs, you have to remove the center clamping piece, flex the panel to install and then reattach the clamping piece. Adjustments to the electric sunroof are covered in the workshop manual. The most common problem is the little ramps on the sides of the sunroof opening are bent and don't allow the legs to push up the sunroof panel. They can be adjusted with pliers. On open cars, now would be the time to install the soft top and/or hard top. This is a two-person job.

When installing the engine, a trick is to weld a small bolt to the heads of the bolts that secure the starter and engine. This will keep the bolts from turning if the engine has to be removed in the future. Alternatively, you can secure a hose clamp to the bolt head. The bolt has to be in place for this option. Behind the engine are two half circle metal pieces that cover where the transmission hoop attaches to the chassis.

When reinstalling scripts on your 356 (hopefully the painter left the holes), the holes will have to be cleaned out with a small file. Mask off the opening and proceed with caution. If for some reason a script hole is too large, you can make a thin shim from an aluminum can and bend it to a small L. Hide the foot of the L behind the script. Attaching clips to the script can be a problem due to the tight space behind the script. You can enlarge the opening on the clip so it just goes on the script stud. Then with the clip captured in a long nose vice grip, attempt to push it on the stud. Once it is on the stud, you can push it flush with a long screwdriver. An alternative is to use small diameter plastic tubing that can be pushed tightly on the stud. Cut it about one-half inch long so it can be pulled off and the script removed for cleaning.

Paint Hardware

Your 356 is now ready for a road test or to go off to the upholstery shop for seat and or panel work, but there is one last item. The factory hand painted many nuts/bolts/washers; some body color, some black. Hopefully, you have some touch-up paint from your painter.

Paint the following body color:
•Nuts/washers under hood handle
•Bolt, washer and nut on front hood hinge
•Door hinge pins (the top pin may have a thin washer and usually a cotter pin)
•Nuts/bolts/washers securing the rear deck
•Door latch screw heads
Paint the following black:
•Rear deck hinge bolts/nuts/washers
•All bumper and bumper bracket bolts/washers
•All exposed hardware under the dash (option)
•Striker plate screws (except 356Cs)

Electrical Connections

When installing the battery ground strap and the ground strap from the transmission to a clean bare metal part of the chassis, use an electrical conductive paste to prevent future corrosion.

Engine

Before replacing the engine, replace the starter bushing. This is in the cup piece of the transmission that receives the starter. Remove the remaining bolt and wires to the starter for access. By replacing this inexpensive, but important, bushing you have one less item to be concerned with if you have starter problems in the future.

Wheels

If you have painted steel wheels, they can be blasted and repainted. A dull aluminum with a clear coat works well;

others prefer various silver colors such as Wurth wheel silver. All the 356 Porsche wheels have a date stamped on them. While it is nice to have wheels with a date close to your month of manufacture, it doesn't add anything to performance and nobody knows unless you make a habit of removing your hubcaps. Chrome wheels with dates can be re-chromed. This involves separating the center, de-chroming and re-chroming and re-welding the center on a special jig. Check the 356 Registry web site for vendors. Wheel size, like shock absorbers and tires, is a personal preference.

Earlier in the three Speedsters story, we mentioned Rudge knock-off wheels. These were optional wheels with a center spinner that were installed/removed with a special hammer. They have become quite valuable. The Rudge wheels on the '55 Speedster in the three Speedsters story were in poor shape. It would cost over $1,000 a wheel to have them professionally restored. We decided on another approach. We had them de-chromed, media blasted and powder painted with a near-chrome finish. They turned out quite well and the cost was under $800 for five wheels.

Turning out the lights! Another enjoyable day of 356 restoration is over.

The End

Wow! You are done with the restoration of a Porsche 356! All that is left is the sorting out and driving enjoyment. Sorting out involves getting all the linkages correct and troubleshooting the electrical system. These procedures are covered in the Workshop Manual and *Restoration Guide*. Before you hit the road to sort out your 356, purchase a halon fire extinguisher. You don't want the powder kind that can damage your engine. Halon fire extinguishers are available from aviation equipment shops and 356 Registry vendors. Also, a final tip, get in the habit of turning off the fuel supply when parking your 356. Turn the petcock handle counterclockwise to ZU. As a reminder that the fuel is turned off, lower your sun visor.

Appendices

Finding a 356
Determining the Value of a Project 356
Sunroof Installation
Nose Replacement
Brakes
Selecting a Painter
Swap Meets
Color Charts
Chassis Number List

Finding a 356

There are still restorable 356s out there. Yes, some are even in barns! Tired and rusty 356s could be bought cheap in the seventies and eighties as restoration projects. Many are still up on blocks in a garage, but the owner never had the time to start or finish the restoration. His job, the kids, the money got in the way.

1957 1500 GS Carrera Coupe #58355

This was our first 356. One of the guys at work with a mutual interest in cars and racing called and said that he had just bought a "Poorsh". He drove it over and the first thing I noticed was that it was right hand drive. The second thing I noticed was the gasoline dripping from a silver thing under the dash and the fact that I could see the road through holes in the floor. He said his Dad could fix the car. We went on a fun drive. This was in 1973.

Five years passed. Jeff had moved to another company, but we were both in an investment club that met monthly. Jeff had told me how his Dad had fixed the floor and fuel leak, but he seldom drove the car. He had married, had kids and the demands of his job had changed his priorities. We were closing out the investment club (very little profit) and I had money in hand and space in the three car garage at our new house. I told Jeff I would buy the 356 for what he had paid for it - $750, but he would have to drive it to my place.

The next weekend Jeff drove it over, with his wife and kids following in the station wagon. He left some Road and Track magazines and said there was an article about the car; it was a Carrera. Now, I didn't know any thing about Porsches and I had a new home to complete, so the car sat for many months. I read the article on the 356 Carrera and my car had the special dash switches but the engine didn't look like the pictures in the article. Eventually, I decided to start the 356 and drive it to a local Porsche dealer for evaluation. I had to call Jeff to find our how to start it since I

The Carrera after the first restoration

didn't know about the switch for the electric fuel pump. The car also would not shut off with the key and I had to kill it with the brake and clutch.

At the dealer they said they wouldn't drive it as the suspension was frozen, the car was full of bondo and rust and they no longer had an ignition switch for that model Porsche. On the way home the hood flew up.

My restoration included having a battery box floor done at the local Vo-Tech, freeing the suspension with numerous applications of WD-40, bondoing the damage in the rear and installing black shag carpet. My son and I painted it black with spray cans. I drove it to work, but had to back into the parking lot because the card reader for entrance was on the left hand side.

Eventually, I realized that I didn't have the skills, time or money to restore this 356 properly, so I decided to trade it. I traded it for a 1963 sunroof coupe from a guy that would restore it and teach me the restoration process. As mentioned elsewhere, I spent a year at the restoration shop

The 1957 1500 GS as it was delivered

The Carrera as restored by the new owner at the Steamboat Springs vintage races. It is still fitted with a pushrod engine

The Carrera as it sits today as a back burner project. The door and lock post have been replaced, as well as the floor pan

assisting in the restoration of the 1963 sunroof coupe which is today my daily driver.

The 1957 1500 GS Carrera was bought by the president of the local region of the Porsche Club of America. He made it into a vintage racer and painted it silver with red racing stripes. It still had a push rod engine. After I moved to Colorado and got active with the Rocky Mountain 356 Porsche Club, I saw the car at a vintage race and told the owner I would like to buy the 356 if it ever was for sale since it was my first Porsche.

Years went by and one day there was a phone call. The 356 was for sale and it now had a Carrera engine! The price was a lot more than the $750 I had originally paid. I discussed it with Barbara and she said "It was your first Porsche. Do It!" So I bought it and as I was now retired and doing 356 restorations, I replaced the floor pan, right side lock post (which were from a later model 356) and the left headlight bucket which had been replaced incorrectly. I also removed the roll bar and the louvers in the rear lid. The car is still a back burner project.

When I bought this 356 the second time, I got the Kardex information with it. It indicated the car had been imported to Bankok Thailand. About a year ago when I mentioned this to a Porsche enthusiast who was visiting the shop, he said, "I wonder if the Prince drove it?" This got my attention and I asked for any information he could find. A week later, he brought over two articles from the 1974 Four Cam Registry. One article was in English and one in Thai. Both mentioned an owner that raced a 1500 GS Carrera in Thailand, but had different names for the owner. I tried an internet search on the names. This was unsuccessful, but I did receive the address of Royal Automobile Association of Thailand. I wrote them a letter requesting any information on the owner on the 356.

A few months later, I received an e-mail from the grandson

of the original owner! While his grandfather had passed on in 1999, his grandmother was alive and had pictures of the car. Yes, his grandfather had raced it and was friends with the Prince, but we don't know if the Prince ever drove the car. The Prince was Prince Bira whose wife Princess Ceril Birabungse wrote a book, *The Prince and I - My Life with Prince Bira of Siam*. The grandson has expressed interest in the 1500GS Carrera and perhaps after we restore it to it's original condition, it will return to Thailand.

1962 Roadster #89621

While working on the restoration of my 1963 sunroof coupe, I was told of a 356B Roadster for sale. Since I now had an interest in these great little cars, I went to look at it. It was in a dark basement shop, was red and looked complete. By flashlight I could see fiberglass had been applied to the body, and it had obviously been stored with chickens. I had been told it was a rare 356 and the asking price was $2,500.00. We agreed on $2,300.00 with delivery to my home across town.

When it arrived it didn't look too bad, but I soon discovered there was fiberglass everywhere. I took pictures, started a project notebook and began disassembly. In those days, media blasting wasn't available and we took the dis-

The Roadster as it arrived and after disassembly

Typical rust damage

The donor chassis

The donor chassis needed much repair but it was made easier by turning the chassis upside down. The suspension also needed adjustment

assembled 356 to a dipper. Soon the phone rang and the dipper said "Jim, your car broke in half." The previous owner had so loved the car he covered it with fiberglass, creating a rust sandwich. When the corrosive solution removed the fiberglass, the 356 came apart in pieces.

This was my first restoration. I had yet to learn how to weld and use body working tools and materials. This

Rebuilding the battery box upside down

restoration took over two years, since I was still working in the computer industry. I put pressure on myself by writing monthly articles for the *Oversteer*, the monthly magazine of the Rocky Mountain 356 Porsche Club. My goal was to finish the restoration and drive the Roadster to the 356 Registry West Coast Holiday the club was hosting in Steamboat Springs, Colorado. This was in August, 1991, and we made it. As mentioned earlier, the twin grille Roadster is the current daily driver of my wife Barbara.

The restoration on this 356 was a major project, one of the most extensive we have ever done. The rear strut area of it was so rusted it had been repaired with fiberglass and 2 x 2 lumber. It was obvious that the bottom of the car was severely rusted. Fortunately we were able to find a chassis from a C Model, but it also had rust damage. We were able to flip the chassis upside down to repair the battery box floor, diagonal, front struts, front closing panels and floor pan. Once this was done, we were able to attach the suspension from the Roadster. Next, we had to attach the Roadster dash and cowl to the hinge posts and front bulkhead of the chassis. We then repaired the doors and hood and attached them. The front fenders and nose had rusted apart and these were repaired on saw horses. It took weeks to align the fenders and nose with the chassis and hood and tack it all into place.

Partial repair of the donor chassis

Fender repair made easier when off the car

Inner fender repair

Using string to line up the pieces

Trial fit of the front of door repair piece

After everything was on the level the hood was used for final alignment

Making sure the door, rocker and repair piece line up

After the front end was assembled, I decided to place the rear end on the car to see how much work it was going to take. It lined right up! The spot weld holes on the rear end lined up with the spot weld locations on the chassis. I tacked it in place. After final welding I spent a lot of time on fit and finish. I used lead to define the contours. This proved to be a problem after the Roadster was painted it's original Ruby Red color. In some areas I had spread the lead beyond the tinned area. Solvents in the paint got under the lead and caused the paint to lift. The Roadster was repainted years later. This problem taught us to only use lead in the areas the factory had used lead. One item I forgot to remove prior to dipping was the chassis ID plate

The Roadster back from the painter. That is Pikes Peak in the background

in the front compartment. Being aluminum, it was destroyed in the dipping process. Years later at a swap meet, in a box of rusty parts, I found an ID plate for a 356B 1600 and three of the numbers matched the Roadster. Using a number punch set of the proper size, I was able to create 89621.

After the major effort to restore the Twin Grille Roadster I had the confidence to restore any 356 and decided to turn my advocation into a vocation when I retired.

Almost together. Installing the wiring harness

Determining the Value of a Project 356

So, you've stumbled over a 356 stored in a barn. It is a project car and you want to determine how much to offer. One method is to research the asking prices for fully restored 356s of the same year/model. With this as a starting point, you can then subtract what it will cost to restore your barn find.

Let's assume the 356 you found was a 1958 coupe without a sunroof (all the Speedsters in a barn may have been discovered). It appears complete but is rusty and tired. The engine supposedly ran when it was stored twenty years ago and still turns over.

So, working backward we research and determine the average price for a restored 1958 coupe is $20,000.00. We do additional research and get restoration cost and parts cost and subtract as follows:

    $20,000.00 - Restored Value
    -       0.00 - Disassembly (do-it-yourself)
    -     800.00 - Media Blasting
    -   5,000.00 - Metal Repair
    -   6,000.00 - Paint
    -     800.00 - Rubber Seals/Mats
    -     500.00 - Windshield
    -   1,200.00 - Chrome
    -   1,500.00 - Parts
    -   3,500.00 - Headliner, Carpet, Interior
    -     500.00 - Paint, Caulk, Undercoat
    -       0.00 - Reassembly (do-it-yourself)
    -   2,000.00 - Contingency
    _____

    ($ 1,800.00)

You are already upside down on this project and you still don't know the condition of the engine or transmission. It would be best not to make an offer on this barn find and look for a 356 in better condition, or plan to do a lot of the work yourself. Now, if the 1958 car you find in the barn is a cabriolet in the same condition, and the average restored value is $35,000.00, you have a viable project.

Often you will find a project 356 with the engine in boxes. Many gearheads buy a project 356 and the first thing they do is disassemble the engine which may or may not have needed disassembly. Next they disassemble the car. Sometimes the parts are properly bagged and marked. Sometimes loose in boxes with masking tape markings which have solidified. To reassemble the engine will take from $3,000.00 to $5,000.00 depending on parts needed. It will be more if you get into the *as long as we're doing this, let's make it something special* mentality. Disassembled engines and 356s should be considered a gamble.

Sunroof Installation

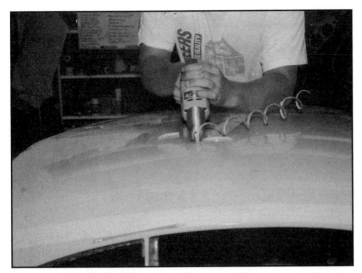

Cutting the hole in the roof for the sunroof. A nervous time after many measurements.

After installation of the sunroof clip it was welded, Seams ground down and leaded.

The opening was flanged and the sun roof clip installed.

Sunroofs were a nice option on 356 coupes. The early sunroofs were mechanical and switched to electrical at about the T-6 model change. The early mechanical sunroofs were V shaped at the front to match the bent windshield. Modifying a non sunroof coupe to receive a sunroof clip from a damaged 356 is a popular modification. The problem is sunroof clips are hard to find and their swap meet value has increased from under a thousand dollars to over three thousand dollars depending on condition.

As mentioned earlier the *Restoration Guide* describes three ways to install a sunroof clip. The pictures here show an installation of just the sunroof, not the complete top. Most of the work on this installation was repairing the clip before installation. It was quite rusty at the brackets that secure it to the roof.

Nose Replacement

The front clip is being removed from this 356 using the plasma cutter. Eye protection is very important when using this tool as the cutting flame can bounce back when it hits thick metal. Note also the battery box floor which had been pop riveted over the rusty original floor. Ledges will be ground off prior to fitting the replacement floor.

The front clip has been removed from this 356 as it was too damaged to repair. The two circles on the front bulkhead are from the factory welding of the jack receivers in the front compartment. Note that these areas have rusted as the factory did not get paint/undercoat up to this area. The lower bulkhead is torn and dented.

The front clip that was removed. It appears to have been hit twice due to the combination of brazing and welding. The Bondo that covered this area was one half inch thick.

The front battery box bulkhead has been replaced at the original seams.

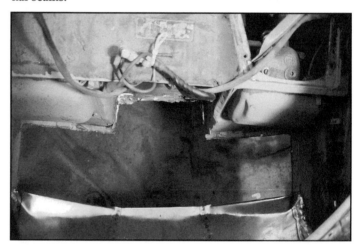

The battery box floor has been removed leaving ledges. The remainder of the original floor on the ledges will be ground off prior to fitting the replacement floor.

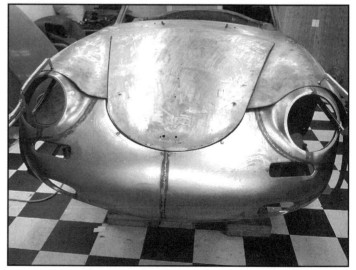

Trial fit of the replacement front clip. The hood and fender braces were used as jigs. Many, many measurements were taken to establish the correct position. When the original front clip was cut off, it was cut short to allow the replacement clip to be positioned under the fenders.

Tack welding the replacement clip. There is a glove on my left hand; the right hand is gloveless to allow better control of the MIG welder trigger.

Getting ready to install a replacement headlight bucket. The bucket had to be modified by removing unnecessary flanges to make it look like a correct 356 headlight bucket.

The front clip tacked in place. The hood used constantly as a jig. Note that the holes for the bumper brackets were not cut in the replacement clip. This was good as the brackets were off center and we were able to cut new holes for their position.

The headlight bucket installed. Note the fender brace protrudes correctly into the bucket. It will be welded and the weld smoothed with two part putty.

Brakes

As you work on the brakes, use every precaution not to get brake fluid on a painted surface. On restorations, we always replace the master cylinder but will restore the wheel cylinders if possible. When working with brake lines and connections, there is a special 11 mm wrench, called a line wrench, with a slot to go over the brake line and capture the connector with more flats than an open-end wrench. They are available at auto parts stores. Clean all connections and use penetrating oil. Bleeder valves in old wheel cylinders have a tendency to break. After removing the wheel cylinder, place it in a vise. Clean around the bleeder valve. Use your penetrating oil. Tap the end of the bleeder valve with a hammer. Tap your 7 mm wrench to tighten, then tap to loosen. Do all this gently. If it doesn't work, apply heat and try again.

To disassemble the wheel cylinder, remove a zerk grease fitting from your front suspension. Screw into wheel cylinder input. Close the bleeder valve and use your grease gun to push out the wheel cylinder components. On rear wheel cylinders, one end may start to move and you will have to hold it to get the other end to move. If one end remains frozen, you will have to use a drift to tap it out, sacrificing a few components, which are easy to replace. Remove all the grease from the wheel cylinder and components. Inspect the wheel cylinder for pitting. If the pits are in the center, the wheel cylinder should be reusable. If pits are at the end, this will not allow the rubber cup to seal and you will have leaks. You need a new or rebuilt wheel cylinder. If the wheel cylinder is reusable, it needs to be honed. Get a VW honing tool at your auto parts store. Place it in a drill and working in a container of brake fluid, hone out the wheel cylinder. Reassemble with new components. While there are other procedures and vendors for disassembly and restoring wheel cylinders, the above procedure has worked for us on over 60 wheel cylinders.

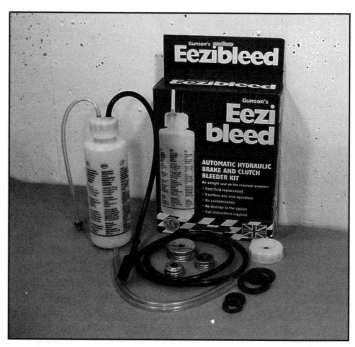

A brake bleeding kit

You need to replace all rubber brake lines. Not a suggestion, a fact. Also inspect all steel lines for wear and damage. Replace as necessary. When making brake line connections, keep all parts as loose as possible to avoid cross threading. If the connection doesn't feel right in the first few threads, stop. Don't force the connections.

Bleeding the brakes can be a two-person job described in many books or a one-person job with a brake bleeding tool. Some tools suck the fluid through the lines, some push the fluid. Most shops have a favorite brake bleeding tool. We use the Eeze Bleed tool. This attaches to a tire with 20 psi and pushes fluid. Very easy to check for leaks at connections before bleeding brakes.

Selecting a Painter

If you do not have painting skills or the time to develop them, you will have to find a painter. The best way is to attend area car shows and ask owners who painted their cars. It does not have to be a Porsche show. With the names of painters you can visit their shops and make a selection. A clean shop with separate areas for prep work and paint is important. The shop does not have to have a high tech paint booth. Some award winning 356s have been painted outside on a gravel bed when there was no wind.

You are going to have to take your 356 to the painter or have him come to you to get an estimate. Have the 356 assembled and clean. If he has not painted a 356 before, point out those areas that are painted but not rubbed out such as the dash top, threshold and hingepost area. If you have sound insulation in the front door cavity, let him know it is not to be painted. If the painter's estimate is acceptable, ask for his terms. Most painters need money up front to buy materials and may want progress payments. Agree up front about quality and the final payment. Also discuss schedule and warranty.

To select the color for your 356, you can take a part with original paint to an automotive paint supply store and have them do a computer match. Most automotive paint stores have hundreds of paint chips that you can also match. "We use one painter who can mix a perfect match by eye". It is not worth the time to try to find the original Porsche formula for your 356's color. Paint products have changed considerably over the last fifty years. It is fun to go to a 356 event and see the differences in the same color, such as Signal Red.

Your painter will have a preference for the paint system he uses be it PPG, Dupont or others. Don't try to make the painter change systems, because you heard something else was best. The painter has to stay within the system including fillers, primers, color to keep the manufacturer's warranty. As paint products have improved over the years, the cost of paint materials have gone up. Paint materials for a 356 will run well over one thousand dollars.

Then there is labor. Prep work is the most time consuming part of the paint process. We used to spend weeks getting a restored 356 body in perfect shape. When we visited our painter he was taking all our hard work off. When we questioned him he said "Hey, I'm responsible for the paint. I want to know what's underneath". During your restoration you made all the gaps correct and flush. Make sure the painter knows not to change your gaps, and if the painter has a helper, make sure the helper knows.

The painter's prep work involves getting the contours of the body to flow. Most of this is done by eye and experience. Your choice of color shouldn't affect the prep work. While white is easy and black and metallics difficult, the prep work should be the same.

Since the painter will paint parts off the 356, make sure he knows how to install the doors, hood and rear lid to insure they fit. Provide the painter with all the parts to be painted so he can purchase the right amount of paint. It's not good if you forget the torsion hole covers and they are painted later and the color doesn't match. Show the painter where the hood and rear deck hinges are painted black and then color, or paint the black area yourself and mask off.

Swap Meets

If you are missing parts for your 356 restoration, put them on a swap meet list. While many parts for the 356 are available from vendors that advertise in the 356 Registry, there are parts that are no longer being manufactured or reproduced. Parts such as radios, interior door handles, rear view mirrors, garnish rails, jacks, early gas tanks and other parts can usually only be found at swap meets or individual for sale ads.

Buying a part without inspecting it first can be a financial disaster. The 356 Registry has a Conditions of Sale/Purchase that protect sellers and buyers who can't preinspect parts. It is safe to buy parts from 356 Registry ads. If you see a part in an ad not in the 356 Registry, ask the vendor if they support the 356 Registry Conditions of Sale/Purchase Conditions. If they don't know these conditions, shop elsewhere.

While the E-Bay auctions on the Internet can be exciting, they can be a problem for the novice 356 parts buyer. It is easy to misrepresent parts on E-Bay; either from lack of knowledge or plain dishonesty. The auction excitement can also push the price of a part beyond reasonableness.

Swap meets are an excellent place to buy 356 parts. There is usually a large swap meet held on each coast once a year; plus local clubs also hold swap meets. Dates for these events can be found in the 356 Registry.

Before attending a swap meet you should do some preparation. Make a list of what you need. Try to determine a fair price for the part by checking ads and asking others. Check *Authenticity* to see if there is a picture of the part. Plan on being at the swap meet at the scheduled start time. This may mean bringing a flashlight! If a vendor isn't busy, read him or show him your list of parts needed to see if they have them. Ask if they know any vendors that might have the parts.

When you find a part, inspect its condition. Does it function? Is it clean? Can it be restored? Is it complete i.e. studs not damaged? Is it for the right or left side? Ask the vendor about the part. Ask others in the area what they think. If you want to buy the part it is okay to dicker with the vendor. They will usually come down in price, particularly if you are buying many parts. If the part is dirty or rusty and you have to restore it, use the condition as a bargaining point.

There is one protocol at a swap meet. Don't ask a vendor to set aside a part while you check out other vendors. This is a courtesy only extended to buyers the vendor knows. When you agree on a price, be prepared to pay cash. Some vendors will take checks if you provide your 356 Registry membership number. Very few vendors are equipped to accept credit cards.

Color Charts

The following color charts are the most accurate and complete available. They are substantially more detailed in the first few years than previously presented. This information has been procured from dealer color listings and factory documentation. There is a lack of consistency in format during the evolution of the 356, but this should not be surprising. With the exception of Speedsters, 1950 - 1955 cars were painted with nitrocellulose lacquer. Speedsters and all 1956 - 1966 cars had enamel finishes. Many of the exterior colors, including the very early ones, can be obtained from suppliers that carry BASF paint, though pigments and materials have changed substantially over the years.

As a rule, most cabriolets had leather seat upholstery. Other models had vinyl with leather optional. Other upholstery, door panels, rear seats etc. were occasionally leather trimmed, as well. U.S. specification cars generally had vinyl inserts on the front seats, while in most other markets cloth/corduroy was predominantly used. Exceptions to this include 1950 - 1952 cars which commonly had cloth seats and door panels, though the storage pockets were vinyl, and the 1953 America series coupes, most of which had simplified corduroy interiors.

1950 - 1952 356

Records of the first few years of production at Porsche are a bit sketchy when it comes to color information. The following is the most recent *accumulation* of the codes and colors for the first three years. Much of this has been assembled by the 356 Porsche Split-Windscreen Register.

The numbers associated with these color listings were in some cases assigned by the coach-builders, Reutter and Gläser. The duplication of colors may be due to this. It is likely that exterior and fabric colors and upholstery materials may have varied over time and between suppliers, as well as between the two coach-builders.

Exterior Colors, Reutter

#	Color
501*	Black
502	Dark Blue
503	Maroon
504*	Ivory
505*	Fish Silver-Grey
506	Moor Green
509	Adria Blue
510*	Radium Green
511*	Light Grey
522*	Azure Blue
523*	Pascha Red
524*	Strawberry Red
526*	Palm Green
527*	Sand Grey
530	Penicillin White (Green?)
531*	Fashion Grey

Exterior Colors, Gläser

The following exterior colors used on Gläser cabriolets and America Roadsters were not used on Reutter cars. The numbers in the Reutter section to the left followed by an asterisk were also used on Gläser cars. All exterior paint used during this time period was lacquer.

White
Flame Red
Rosede Green
Red (#946 Glasso)
Sand Beige
Persian Blue

Standard Exterior Colors (Reutter July 1951)

Coupe

#	Color
501	Black
503	Maroon
504	Ivory
505	Fish Silver-Grey
506	Moor Green
509	Adria Blue
510	Radium Green

Cabriolet

#	Color
501	Black
522	Azure Blue
523	Pascha Red
524	Strawberry Red
526	Palm Green
527	Sand Grey
531	Fashion Grey

Upholstery – Cloth

Generally, this was corduroy or other textured cloth. It may have been used in combination with other cloth or vinyl.

3287	Green
3323	Beige-Rosé
3325	Brown
3326	Blue
3328	Blue
3361	Grey
3362	Beige
3363	Maroon
5287	Russ Green
?	Olive Green

Additionally, various plaid and checked cloths were offered.

Upholstery – Vinyl (leatherette)

145	Yellow Earth, ochre
309	Dark Blue
310	Blue-Grey
319	?
325	Grey-Green "leather"
335	Red (special)
356	Red
357	Green
358	Brown "textured"
359	Brown "leather"
365	Grey
366	Light Beige
368	Grey
378	Red, Rosanil brand
3090	Blue

Upholstery – Leather

2150	Red
2152	Blue
2153	Hound's Tooth (light grey w/ black highlights)
2154	Light Beige
2155	Dark Green
2161	Grey
2164	Beige
2169	Brown
2180	Beige-Rosé

Headliner & Side Upholstery

511	Beige
512	Blue-Grey
3256	Brown?
3292	Black?
3288	Green
3360	Tan/Beige
3364	Blue-Grey, napped cloth
3365	Tan, napped cloth
3366	Brown?
3367	?

Carpet – Velour

685	Blue
691	Green
692	Tan/Brown

Carpet – Square Weave, Bouclé

678	Blue
679	Light Grey
680	Green
687	?
695	Beige
697	Dark Tan
803	?

Top & Tonneau, Cabriolet

100	Beige
110	Beige-Rosé
521	Grey-Blue
5101	Black
5102	Dark Blue
5106	Grey
5108	Beige
5109	Brown
5111	Blue-Grey
6325	Gray-Green

1953

The following information was collected from an undated dealer sample book. Based on the limited selections, we have surmised that it is from 1953, although other combinations from the previous page are potentially correct for this model year. With the exception of the exterior color names, which are the actual Porsche/Reutter names, the other colors are descriptive, based on their appearance in the sample book. No color numbers were listed other than color package number listed at the left.

Coupe

Reutter #	Color	Vinyl	Cloth
R501CS	Black	tan textured vinyl speckled w/ brown dots	tan corduroy
R501B	Black	reddish brown vinyl	no cloth
R501C	Black	medium dark green textured vinyl	no cloth
R504A	Ivory	reddish brown vinyl	no cloth
R504B	Ivory	medium dark green textured vinyl	no cloth
R510CS	Radium Green	tan textured vinyl speckled w/ brown dots	tan corduroy
R523CS	Pascha Red	tan textured vinyl speckled w/ brown dots	tan corduroy
R523B	Pascha Red	grey heavily textured vinyl	no cloth
R526CS	Palm Green	tan textured vinyl speckled w/ brown dots	tan corduroy
R526B	Palm Green	"oyster" white heavily textured vinyl	no cloth
R531CS	Fashion Grey	grey textured vinyl speckled w/ grey dots	grey corduroy

Cabriolet

Reutter #	Color	Interior (leather)	Top
C501A	Black	reddish brown	tan
C501B	Black	medium dark green	tan
C501C	Black	light tan	tan
C522A	Azure Blue	light tan	tan
C522B	Azure Blue	grey	grey
C523A	Pascha Red	light tan	tan
C524A	Strawberry Red	light tan	tan
C524B	Strawberry Red	black	grey
C526A	Palm Green	light tan	tan
C527A	Sand Grey	reddish brown	mahogany
C531A	Fashion Grey	grey/blue	dark blue
C531B	Fashion Grey	reddish brown	black

Optional leather:

2150 reddish brown	2152 grey/blue	2153 grey
2154 light tan	2155 med dark green	

1954 - 1955 356

Porsche #	Reutter #	Exterior Color *	Coupe Upholstery (leatherette)	Knobs	Cabriolet Upholstery (leather)	Carpet	Lugg. comp.	Headliner	Top/Boot
5401	501	Black	A beige w/ cord. inserts B red or green	beige beige	A red Rosanil 378 B green 2155 C beige	beige 2505 green beige	red vinyl green vinyl beige vinyl	beige rosé 3360 green beige	beige 5108 beige 5108 beige 5108
5402	538	Turkish Red	A beige w/ beige cord. B yellow	beige beige	beige rosé 2180	beige	beige vinyl	beige rosé	beige rosé 110
5403	537	Graphite Metallic	A beige w/ beige cord. B yellow	beige beige	beige 2164	beige	beige vinyl	beige	beige 5108
5404	504	Ivory	A green w/ beige cord. B red w/ beige cord. also red or green	beige beige beige					
5405	536	Jade Green Metallic	A yellow w/ beige cord. B yellow	beige beige	beige 2164	beige	beige vinyl	beige	gray/green C 6325
5406	535	Silver Metallic	A red w/ grey cord. B red or green	grey grey	red Rosanil 378	grey 679	red vinyl	grey	black 5101
5407	534	Pearl Grey	A blue w/ grey cord. B red	grey grey	blue 2152	blue 678	blue vinyl	grey	grey/blue 521
5408	522	Azure Blue	A grey w/ grey cord. B yellow	grey beige	grey 2161	grey 679	grey vinyl	grey	grey 5106
5409	533	Terra Cotta			yellow earth 145	terracotta 363	yellow earth	yellow earth	beige 100
(from September 1954) 5410	509	Adria Blue Metallic	A grey w/ grey cord. B wine red or blue	grey grey					

Speedster

Porsche #	Reutter #	Exterior Color *	Upholstery (leatherette)	Carpet	Top
—	601	Signal Red (Fire Red)	Acella bast (basket-weave) cream black	tan dark tan w/ black vinyl binding	tan black
—	602	Speedster Blue (Sky Blue)	Acella bast (basket-weave) cream	tan	tan
—	603	White	black red	dark tan w/ black vinyl binding red	black black

* Coupe and cabriolet exterior paint was nitrocellulose lacquer. Speedster colors were enamel.

1956 356A

Coupe

Porsche #	Reutter #	Exterior Color*	Upholstery (leatherette)	Dashboard Paint	Dashboard Upholstery	Cabriolet Upholstery (leather)	Cabriolet Dashboard Paint	Cabriolet Dashboard Upholstery
5601	701	Black	A beige w/ beige cord. inserts B red C green	beige beige beige	black black black	A beige B green C red	black black black	black green black
5602	604	Polyantha Red	A beige w/ beige cord. inserts B Naturbast beige**	Polyantha Polyantha	dark red dark red	beige	Polyantha	dark red
5603	737	Graphite Metallic	beige w/ viscose silk fabric	beige	graphite	beige	Graphite	graphite
5604	605	Sahara Beige	A Carskin 132 beige comb. B red	red beige	dark red dark red	red	red	red
5605	606	Lago Green Metallic	A Carskin 132 beige comb.*** B Carskin 133 beige comb.	Lago Green Lago Green	dark green dark green	beige	Lago Green	dark green
5606	608	Silver Metallic	A red B green	silver silver	dark red green	A red B green	red dark green	red green
5607	607	Aquamarine Blue Metallic	A red B grey w/ grey cord. inserts	red Aquamarine	dark red blue	A grey B red	blue red	dark blue dark red

Cabriolet (right-hand section of the table, columns for Upholstery (leather) and Dashboard)

* As of the 1956 model year, all exterior paint was enamel
** Available in beige leatherette without charge
*** Viscose silk fabric

1957 - 1959 356A

Porsche #	Reutter #	Exterior Color	**Coupe** Upholstery (leatherette)	**Cabriolet** Dashboard	Upholstery (leather seats)	**Speedster** Top	Upholstery (leatherette)
5701	701	Black	A red / A/C red w/ red cord. inserts / B beige / B/C beige w/ beige cord. inserts	red / black	A red / B beige	beige / black	A red / B beige
5702	702	Ruby Red	A beige / A/C beige w/ beige cord. inserts / B brown / B/C brown w/ brown cord. inserts	red	A beige / B brown	black / black	A tan / B black
5703	703	Meissen Blue	A red / A/C red w/ red cord. inserts / B brown / B/C brown w/ brown cord. inserts	red / brown	A red / B brown	black / black	A red / B black
5704	704	Ivory	A red / A/C red w/ red cord. inserts / B brown / B/C brown w/ brown cord. inserts	red / brown	A red / B brown	black / black	A red / B black
5705	705	Fjord Green	A beige / A/C beige w/ beige cord. inserts / B brown / B/C brown w/ brown cord. inserts	brown	A beige	beige	A brown / B tan
5706	608	Silver Metallic	A red / A/C red w/ red cord. inserts / B green / B/C green w/ green cord. inserts	red / green	A red / B green	black / black	A red / B black
5707	707	Aquamarine Blue	A red / A/C red w/ red cord. inserts / B brown / B/C brown w/ brown cord. inserts	red / brown	A red / B brown	black	A red / B light brown

SPECIAL PAINTS:

Porsche #	Reutter #	Exterior Color	**Coupe** Upholstery (leatherette)	**Cabriolet** Dashboard	Upholstery (leather seats)	**Speedster** Top	Upholstery (leatherette)
5710	710	Stone Grey	A red / A/C red w/ red cord. inserts / B brown / B/C brown w/ brown cord. inserts	red / brown	A red / B brown	black / black	A red / B black
5711	711	Orange	A beige / A/C beige w/ beige cord. inserts / B black	brown / black	A black	black	A light brown
5712	712	Auratium Green	A beige / A/C beige w/ beige cord. inserts / B brown / B/C brown w/ brown cord. inserts	black / brown	A beige	beige	B black / A beige
5713	713	Glacier White	B brown / B/C brown w/ brown cord. inserts / B green / B/C green w/ green cord. inserts	brown / green	A black / B green	black / black	B brown / B black

94

Porsche #	Reutter #	Exterior Color	Coupe & Hardtop — Upholstery (leatherette)	Cabriolet & Roadster — Upholstery (leather seats for cabriolets)
6001	741	Slate Grey	A red A/C red w/ "Bordeaux" cord. inserts D light grey D/C light grey w/ "Stone" cord. inserts	A red D light grey
6002	702	Ruby Red	C light brown C/C light brown w/ "Birch" cord. inserts D light grey D/C light grey w/ "Stone" cord. inserts	C light brown D light grey
6003	740	Aetna Blue	A red A/C red w/ "Bordeaux" cord. inserts D light grey D/C light grey w/ "Stone" cord. inserts	A red D light grey
6004	738	Ivory	A red A/C red w/ "Bordeaux" cord. inserts B black B/C black w/ "Mouse" cord. inserts C light brown C/C light brown w/ "Birch" cord. inserts D light grey D/C light grey w/ "Stone" cord. inserts	A red B black C light brown D light grey
6005	705	Fjord Green	A red A/C red w/ "Bordeaux" cord. inserts F blue F/C blue w/ "Pearl" cord. inserts	A red F blue
6006	608	Silver Metallic	A red A/C red w/ "Bordeaux" cord. inserts F blue F/C blue w/ "Pearl" cord. inserts	A red F blue
6007	639	Heron Grey	B black B/C black w/ "Mouse" cord. inserts E dark grey E/C dar grey w/ "Stone" cord. inserts	B black E dark grey

SPECIAL PAINTS:

Porsche #	Reutter #	Exterior Color	Coupe & Hardtop — Upholstery (leatherette)	Cabriolet & Roadster — Upholstery (leather seats for cabriolets)
6010	743	Condor Yellow	B black B/C black w/ "Mouse" cord. inserts E dark grey E/C dar grey w/ "Stone" cord. inserts	B black E dark grey
6011	601	Signal Red	B black B/C black w/ "Mouse" cord. inserts D light grey D/C light grey w/ "Stone" cord. inserts	B black D light grey
6012	742	Royal Blue	B black B/C black w/ "Mouse" cord. inserts D light grey D/C light grey w/ "Stone" cord. inserts	B black D light grey
6013	701	Black	A red A/C red w/ "Bordeaux" cord. inserts C light brown C/C light brown w/ "Birch" cord. inserts	A red C light brown

1962 - 1963 356B

Coupe & Hardtop
Upholstery (leatherette)

Cabriolet & Roadster
Upholstery (leather seats for cabriolets)

Porsche #	Reutter #	Exterior Color	Coupe & Hardtop Upholstery (leatherette)	Cabriolet & Roadster Upholstery (leather)
6201	741	Slate Grey	A red A/C red w/ red cord. inserts G green G/C green w/ green cord. inserts	A red G green
6202	702	Ruby Red	B black B/C black w/ Mouse Grey cord. inserts D grey D/C grey w/ Pearl Grey cord. insrets	B black D grey
6203	745	Oslo Blue	A red A/C red w/ red cord. inserts D grey D/C grey w/ Pearl Grey cord. insrets H brown	A red D grey H brown
6204	738	Ivory	H brown H/C brown w/ brown cord. inserts A red A/C red w/ red cord. inserts	A red
6205	747	Champagne Yellow	G green G/C green w/ green cord. inserts B black B/C black w/ Mouse Grey cord. inserts	G green B black
6206	608	Silver Metallic	A red A/C red w/ red cord. inserts F blue F/C blue w/ Pearl Grey cord. inserts	A red F blue
6207	739	Heron Grey	G green G/C green w/ green cord. inserts H brown H/C brown w/ brown cord. inserts	G green H brown
SPECIAL PAINTS:				
6210	744	Smyrna Green	H brown H/C brown w/ brown cord. inserts D grey D/C grey w/ Pearl Grey cord. insrets	H brown D grey
6211	601	Signal Red	B black B/C black w/ Mouse Grey cord. inserts D grey D/C grey w/ Pearl Grey cord. inserts	B black D grey
6212	746	Bali Blue	C light brown C/C light brown w/ light brown cord. inserts D grey D/C grey w/ Pearl Grey cord. inserts	C light brown D grey
6213	701	Black	A red A/C red w/ red cord. inserts G green G/C green w/ green cord. inserts	A red G green

1964 - 1965 356C

Coupe — Upholstery (leatherette)

Cabriolet — Upholstery (leather seats)

Porsche #	Reutter #	Exterior Color	Coupe Upholstery (leatherette)	Cabriolet Upholstery (leather seats)
6401	—	Slate Grey	A red A/C red w/ red cord. inserts K fawn K/C fawn w/ fawn cord. inserts	A red K fawn
6402	—	Ruby Red	B black B/C black w/ Mouse Grey cord. inserts D grey D/C grey w/ Pearl Grey cord. insrets	B black D grey
6403	—	Sky Blue	A red A/C red w/ red cord. inserts K fawn K/C fawn w/ fawn cord. inserts	A red K fawn
6404	—	Light Ivory	A red A/C red w/ red cord. inserts B black B/C black w/ Mouse Grey cord. inserts G green G/C green w/ green cord. inserts	A red B black G green
6405	—	Champagne Yellow	B black B/C black w/ Mouse Grey cord. inserts K fawn K/C fawn w/ fawn cord. inserts D grey D/C grey w/ Pearl Grey cord. inserts	B black K fawn D grey
6406	—	Irish Green	B black B/C black w/ Mouse Grey cord. inserts K fawn K/C fawn w/ fawn cord. inserts D grey D/C grey w/ Pearl Grey cord. insrets	B black K fawn D grey
6407	—	Signal Red	B black B/C black w/ Mouse Grey cord. inserts D grey D/C grey w/ Pearl Grey cord. insrets	B black D grey
SPECIAL PAINTS:				
6410	—	Dolphin Grey	F blue F/C blue w/ Pearl Grey cord. insrets G green G/C green w/ green cord. inserts	F blue G green
6411	—	Togo Brown	G green G/C green w/ green cord. inserts K fawn K/C fawn w/ fawn cord. inserts	G green K fawn
6412	—	Bali Blue	K fawn K/C fawn w/ fawn cord. inserts D grey D/C grey w/ Pearl Grey cord. insrets	K fawn D grey
6413	—	Black	A red A/C red w/ red cord. inserts G green G/C green w/ green cord. inserts	A red G green

Chassis Number List

Chassis numbers can be misleading. The number indicates the order in which the chassis was constructed, but not the order in which the car was completed or sold. Due to damage during assembly or component failures, cars many months out of sequence were completed and potentially fitted with trim and mechanical items that were used on cars being finished along side them. Cars built toward the end of a model year are frequently officially included in the next year's production. When a major change occurred, such as 356 to 356A, some unusual permutations were created. For example, 1955 356 Speedsters fitted with 1600 engines, which were manufactured for several months alongside 356A coupes and cabriolets. While these cars lead to confusion and controversy, it is not difficult to understand why they exist. It should be noted, however, that they are the exception, not the rule.

Engine numbers are also a bit troubling for some of the same reasons listed above. The numbers on the list should be considered relative. This is especially true at the beginning and end of a model or calendar year. The only way to verify which engine was fitted to which chassis is to examine the original factory records. For a fee, this service is provided to owners of 356s by Porsche Cars North America. For additional information contact: Certificate of Authenticity Program, Attention: Barbara Kurz, 1929 Mountain Industrial Boulevard, Tucker, GA 30084, Phone 404-557-3451, FAX 770-723-0244. e-mail: bkurz@sspci.com

For years, the chassis number list that was contained in the Porsche Spec's book was the the gospel according to Porsche. In the early 1990s with the help of Olaf Lang at Porsche AG and Marco Marinello, the following, more accurate list was compiled. It contains the several additional series of cars, Carrera engine types and exchange chassis numbers. It is interesting to note that some of the latter are duplicates of 1952 cabriolet numbers. A number of gaps in numerical series are not seen in the original Porsche list. Several typographical errors have been corrected, as well as adding and subtracting chassis numbers where appropriate.

Year Mfg		Vehicle and Engine Model Designation	Engine Model	Crank-case	Carburetors	Stroke/ Bore	Compr. Ratio	HP (DIN) @ RPM	Engine Serial #
1950		**(356)** 356/1100	369	2 PB	32 PBI	64/73.5	7:1	40 @ 4200	0101 - 0411
1951		356/1100	369	2 PB	32 PBI	64/73.5	7:1	40 @ 4200	0412 - 0999
									10001 - 10137
		356/1300	506	2 PB	32 PBI	64/80	6.5:1	44 @ 4200	1001 - 1099
									20001 - 20821
	from Oct.	356/1500	527	2 RB	40 PBIC	74/80	7:1	60 @ 5000	30001 - 30737
1952		356/1100	369	2 PB	32 PBI	64/73.5	7:1	40 @ 4200	10138 - 10151
		356/1300	506	2 PB	32 PBI	64/80	6.5:1	44 @ 4200	20822 - 21297
	until Nov.	356/1500	527	2 RB	40 PBIC	74/80	7:1	60 @ 5000	30738 - 30750
	from Aug.	356/1500	546	2 PB	32 PBI	74/80	7:1	55 @ 4400	30751 - 31025
	from July	356/1500 S	528	2 RB	40 PBIC	74/80	8.2:1	70 @ 5000	40001 - 40117
1953		356/1100	369	2 PB	32 PBI	64/73.5	7:1	40 @ 4200	10152 - 10161
		356/1300	506	2 PB	32 PBI	64/80	6.5:1	44 @ 4200	21298 - 21636
		356/1500	546	2 PB	32 PBI	74/80	7:1	55 @ 4400	31026 - 32569
		356/1500 S	528	2 RB	40 PBIC	74/80	8.2:1	70 @ 5000	40118 - 40685
	from Sept.	356/1300 S	589	2 RB	32 PBI	74/74.5	8.2:1	60 @ 5500	50001 - 50017
1954		356/1100	369	2 PB	32 PBI	64/73.5	7:1	40 @ 4200	10162 - 10199
		356/1300	506	2 PB	32 PBI	64/80	6.5:1	44 @ 4200	21637 - 21780
	until Nov.	356/1300 S	589	2 RB	32 PBI	74/74.5	8.2:1	60 @ 5500	50018 - 50099
	July to Nov.	356/1300 A	506/1	2 PB	32 PBI	74/74.5	6.5:1	44 @ 4200	21781 - 21999
	until Dec.	356/1500	546	2 PB	32 PBI	74/80	7:1	55 @ 4400	32570 - 33899
	until Dec.	356/1500 S	528	2 RB	40 PICB	74/80	8.2:1	70 @ 5000	40686 - 40999
	From Nov.	356/1300	506/2	3 PB	32 PBI	74/74.5	6.5:1	44 @ 4200	22001 - 22021
	From Dec.	356/1300 S	589/2	3 RB	32 PBIC +	74/74.5	7.5:1	60 @ 5500	50101 - 50127
		356/1500	546/2	3 PB	32 PBI	74/80	7:1	55 @ 4400	33901 - 34119
		356/1500 S	528/2	3 RB	40 PICB	74/80	8.2:1	70 @ 5000	41001 - 41048
1955	until Oct.	356/1300	506/2	3 PB	32 PBI	74/74.5	6.5:1	44 @ 4200	22022 - 22245
		356/1300 S	589/2	3 RB	32 PBIC +	74/74.5	7.5:1	60 @ 5500	50101 - 50127
	from July	Carrera 1500	547	RB	40 PII-4	66/85	9.5:1	110 @ 6200	90001 - 90096
		356/1500	546/2	3 PB	32 PBI	74/80	7:1	55 @ 4400	34120 - 35790
		356/1500 S	528/2	3 RB	40 PICB	74/80	8.2:1	70 @ 5000	41049 - 41999
	from Oct.	356A/1300	506/2	3 PB	32 PBI	74/74.5	6.5:1	44 @ 4200	22246 - 22273
	(356A)	356A/1300 S	589/2	3 RB	32 PBIC +	74/74.5	7.5:1	60 @ 5500	50128 - 50135
	from Nov.	Carrera 1500 GS	547/1	RB	40 PII-4	66/85	9.0:1	100 @ 6200	90501 - 90959
		Carrera 1500 GT	547/1	RB	40 PII-4	66/85	9.0:1	110 @ 6200	90501 - 90959
	from Oct.	356A/1600	616/1	3 PB	32 PBIC	74/82.5	7.5:1	60 @ 4500	60001 - 60608
	from Sept.	356A/1600 S	616/2	3 RB	40 PICB	74/82.5	8.5:1	75 @ 5000	80001 - 80110
1956		356A/1300	506/2	3 PB	32 PBI	74/74.5	6.5:1	44 @ 4200	22274 - 22471
		356A/1300 S	589/2	3 RB	32 PBIC +	74/74.5	7.5:1	60 @ 5500	50136 - 50155
		Carrera 1500 GS	547/1	RB	40 PII-4	66/85	9.0:1	100 @ 6200	90501 - 90959
		Carrera 1500 GT	547/1	RB	40 PII-4	66/85	9.0:1	110 @ 6200	90501 - 90959
		356A/1600	616/1	3 PB	32 PBIC	74/82.5	7.5:1	60 @ 4500	60609 - 63926
		356A/1600 S	616/2	3 RB	40 PICB	74/82.5	8.5:1	75 @ 5000	80111 - 80756

Reutter Coupe	Karmann Coupe	Karmann Hardtop	Reutter Cabriolet	Gläser Cabriolet	Speedster		Model Years
5002 - 5013 5017 - 5018 5020 - 5026 5029 - 5032 5034 - 5104 5163 - 5410			5014 - 5015 5033 5115 5131	5001 5019 5027 - 5028 5105 - 5114 5116 - 5130			1950
5411 - 5600			5132 - 5138	5139 - 5162			
10531 - 11280			10001 - 10165	10351 - 10432			Model 51
11301 - 11360			10166 - 10211 10251 - 10270	10433 - 10469			
11361 - 11778			10271 - 10350 15001 - 15050	12301 - 12387			Model 52
11779 -12084 50001 - 51231			15051 - 15116 60001 - 60394	The two above series include all America Roadsters			1953 Model
51232 - 52029			60395 - 60549				
52030 - 52844			60550 - 60693				1954 Model
52845 - 53008			60694 - 60722		80001 - 80200 (12223 = 80001)		1955 Model
53009 - 54223			60723 - 60923		80201 - 81234		
55001 - 55390			61001 - 61069				
55391 - 58311			61070 - 61499		82001 - 83156		

Year Mfg		Vehicle and Engine Model Designation	Engine Model	Crank-case	Carburetors	Stroke/ Bore	Compr. Ratio	HP (DIN) @ RPM	Engine Serial #
1957	until Aug.	356A/1300	506/2	3 PB	32 PBI	74/74.5	6.5:1	44 @ 4200	22472 - 22999
		356A/1300 S	589/2	3 RB	32 PBIC +	74/74.5	7.5:1	60 @ 5500	50156 - 50999
		Carrera 1500 GS	547/1	RB	40 PII-4	66/85	9.0:1	100 @ 6200	90501 - 90959
		Carrera 1500 GT	547/1	RB	40 PII-4	66/85	9.0:1	110 @ 6200	90501 - 90959
		356A/1600	616/1	3 PB	32 PBIC	74/82.5	7.5:1	60 @ 4500	63927 - 66999
		356A/1600S	616/2	3 RB	40 PICB	74/82.5	8.5:1	75 @ 5000	80757 - 81199
	from Sept. (356A T 2)	Carrera 1500 GS	547/1	RB	40 PII-4	66/85	9.0:1	100 @ 6200	90501 - 90959
		Carrera 1500 GT	547/1	RB	40 PII-4	66/85	9.0:1	110 @ 6200	90501 - 90959
		356A/1600	616/1	3 PB	32 NDIX	74/82.5	7.5:1	60 @ 4500	67001 - 68216
		356A/1600 S	616/2	3 PB	32 NDIX	74/82.5	8.5:1	75 @ 5000	81201 - 81521
1958		356A/1600	616/1	3 PB	32 NDIX	74/82.5	7.5:1	60 @ 4500	68217 - 72468
		356A/1600 S	616/2	3 PB	32 NDIX	74/82.5	8.5:1	75 @ 5000	81522 - 83145
	from May	Carrera 1500 GT	692/0	RB	40 PII-4	66/85	9.0:1	110 @ 6400	91001 - 91037
			692/1	PB	40 PII-4	66/85	9.0:1	110 @ 6400	92001 - 92014
	from Aug.	Carrera 1600 GS	692/2	PB	40 PII-4	66/87.5	9.5:1	105 @ 6500	93001 - 93065
1959	from Feb.	Carrera 1600 GT	692/3	PB	W 40 DCM	66/87.5	9.8:1	115 @ 6500	95001 - 95114
	until Sept.	356A/1600	616/1	3 PB	32 NDIX	74/82.5	7.5:1	60 @ 4500	72469 - 79999
		356A/1600 S	616/2	3 PB	32 NDIX	74/82.5	8.5:1	75 @ 5000	83146 -84770
	from Sept. (356B T 5)	356B/1600	616/1	3 PB	32 NDIX	74/82.5	7.5:1	60 @ 4500	600101 - 601500
		356B/1600 S	616/2	3 PB	32 NDIX	74/82.5	8.5:1	75 @ 5000	84771 - 85550
		356B/1600 S-90	616/7	3 PB	40 PII-4	74/82.5	9:1	90 @ 5500	800101 - 802000
		Carrera 1600 GS	692/2	PB	40 PII-4	66/87.5	9.5:1	105 @ 6500	93101 - 93138
		Carrera 1600 GT	692/3	PB	W 40 DCM	66/87.5	9.8:1	115 @ 6500	95001 - 95114
1960		356B/1600	616/1	3 PB	32 NDIX	74/82.5	7.5:1	60 @ 4500	601501 - 604700
		356B/1600 S	616/2	3 PB	32 NDIX	74/82.5	8.5:1	75 @ 5000	85551 - 88320
		356B/1600 S-90	616/7	3 PB	40 PII-4	74/82.5	9:1	90 @ 5500	800101 - 802000
		Carrera 1600 GT	692/3	PB	W 40 DCM	66/87.5	9.8:1	115 @ 6500	95001 - 95114
			692/3A	PB	44 PII-4	66/87.5	9.8:1	134 @ 7300	96001 - 96050
1961	until Sept.	356B/1600	616/1	3 PB	32 NDIX	74/82.5	7.5:1	60 @ 4500	604701 - 606799
		356B/1600 S	616/2	3 PB	32 NDIX	74/82.5	8.5:1	75 @ 5000	88321 - 89999
									085001 - 085670
		356B/1600 S-90	616/7	3 PB	40 PII-4	74/82.5	9:1	90 @ 5500	802001 - 803999
		Carrera 1600 GT	692/3A	PB	44 PII-4	66/87.5	9.8:1	134 @ 7300	96001 - 96050
	from Sept.	356B/1600	616/1	3 PB	32 NDIX	74/82.5	7.5:1	60 @ 4500	606801 - 607750
	from Aug.	356B/1600 S	616/12	3 PB	32 NDIX	74/82.5	8.5:1	75 @ 5000	700001 - 701200
	(356B T 6)	356B/1600 S-90	616/7	3 PB	40 PII-4	74/82.5	9:1	90 @ 5500	804001 - 804630
1962	until July	356B/1600	616/1	3 PB	32 NDIX	74/82.5	7.5:1	60 @ 4500	607751 - 608900
		356B/1600 S	616/12	3 PB	32 NDIX	74/82.5	8.5:1	75 @ 5000	701201 - 702800
		356B/1600 S-90	616/7	3 PB	40 PII-4	74/82.5	9:1	90 @ 5500	804631 - 805600
		Carrera 2/2000 GS	587/1	PB	40 PII-4	74/92	9.2:1	130 @ 6200	97001 - 97446
	from July	356B/1600	616/1	3 PB	32 NDIX	74/82.5	7.5:1	60 @ 4500	608901 - 610000
		356B/1600 S	616/12	3 PB	32 NDIX	74/82.5	8.5:1	75 @ 5000	702801 - 705050
		356B/1600 S-90	616/7	3 PB	40 PII-4	74/82.5	9:1	90 @ 5500	805601 - 806600

Reutter Coupe	Karmann Coupe	Karmann Hardtop	Reutter Cabriolet	Gläser Cabriolet	Speedster	Convertible D	Roadster
58312 - 59099 100001 - 101692			61500 - 61892		83201 - 83791		
101693 - 102504			150001 - 150149		83792 - 84370		
102505 - 106174			150150 - 151531		84371 - 84922	85501 - 85886	
106175 - 108917			151532 - 152475		84923 - 84954	85887 - 86830	
108918 - 110237			152476 - 152943				86831 - 87391
110238 - 114650			152944 - 154560				87392 - 88920
114651 - 117476		200001 - 201048	154561 - 155569				88921 - 89010 Drauz 89011 - 89483 D'Ieteren
117601 - 118950		201601 - 202200	155601 - 156200				89601 - 89849
118951 - 121099	210001 - 210899	202201 - 202299	156201 - 156999				
121100 - 123042	210900 - 212171		157000 - 157768				

Year Mfg	Vehicle and Engine Model Designation		Engine Model	Crank-case	Carburetors	Stroke/ Bore	Compr. Ratio	HP (DIN) @ RPM	Engine Serial #
1963	until July	356B/1600	616/1	3 PB	32 NDIX	74/82.5	7.5:1	60 @ 4500	610001 - 611000 0600501 - 0600600 611001 - 611200*
		356B/1600 S	616/12	3 PB	32 NDIX	74/82.5	8.5:1	75 @ 5000	705051 - 706000 0700501 - 0701200 706001 - 707200*
		356B/1600 S-90	616/7	3 PB	40 PII-4	74/82.5	9:1	90 @ 5500	806601 - 807000 0800501 - 0801000 807001 - 807400*
		Carrera 2/2000 GS	587/1	PB	40 PII-4	74/92	9.2:1	130 @ 6200	97001 - 97446
		Carrera 2/2000 GT	587/2	PB	W 46 IDM/2	74/92	9.8:1	160 @ 6900	98001 - 98032
	from July **(356C)**	356C/1600 C	616/15	3 PB	32 NDIX	74/82.5	8.5:1	75 @ 5200	710001 - 711870 730001 - 731102* 810001 - 811001 820001 - 820522*
		356C/1600 SC	616/16	3 PB	40 PII-4	74/82.5	9.5:1	95 @ 5800	
1964		356C/1600 C	616/15	3 PB	32 NDIX	74/82.5	8.5:1	75 @ 5200	711871 - 716804 731103 - 733027* 811002 - 813562 820523 - 821701*
		356C/1600 SC	616/16	3 PB	40 PII-4	74/82.5	9.5:1	95 @ 5800	
		Carrera 2/2000 GS	587/1	PB	40 PII-4	74/92	9.2:1	130 @ 6200	97001 - 97446
1965		356C/1600 C	616/15	3 PB	32 NDIX	74/82.5	8.5:1	75 @ 5200	716805 - 717899 733028 - 733197* 813563 - 813893 821702 - 821855*
		356C/1600 SC	616/16	3 PB	40 PII-4	74/82.5	9.5:1	95 @ 5800	
1966	March	356C/1600 SC	616/26	3 PB	40 PII-4	74/82.5	9.5:1	95 @ 5800	813894 - 813903

PB: Plain journal bearings   2: Two-piece crankcase   + 589/2 1300S engines were also equipped   * equipped with new heater system
RB: Roller bearings   3: Three-piece crankcase   with 40 PICB carburetors

Reutter Coupe	Karmann Coupe	Karmann Hardtop	Reutter Cabriolet	Gläser Cabriolet	Speedster	Convertible D	Roadster
123043 - 125246	212172 - 214400		157769 - 158700				
126001 - 128104	215001 - 216738		159001 - 159832				
128105 - 131927	216739 - 221482		159833 - 161577				
131928 - 131930	221483 - 222580		161578 - 162165				
			162166 - 162175				

Additionally there were three series of *exchange chassis* for various cars, including race cars, prototypes, damaged customer cars, Abarth vehicles, South African built cabriolets and random production cars. These numbers do not correlate to any particular model or type.

Years Mfg.	Chassis Number
1953 - 1961	12201 - 12376
1958 - 1962	5601 - 5624
1959 - 1965	13001 - 13414